Tidings Out of the East

Other Books by David Arthur Miller

Restoring the Holy of Holies - Revelation - A Seven-act Play

Omega Now - A Most Startling Heresy

Restoring Ta Hagia - Recreating the Image of God in His People

Prophetic Secrets and the New World Order
(Print only)

Bible Prophecy and Globalism
(Kindle only)

Copyright 2013 David Arthur Miller

All rights reserved

ISBN-13 978-0615738017
ISBN-10 06157801X

Tidings Out of the East

A Commentary on Daniel 10-12

David Arthur Miller

This book is dedicated to the students of my Bible class. They give me reason to study and write. They're a great encouragement to me, inspiring me to present the Living Word in the Present Truth, the only hope for the faint and the weary.

Table of Contents

Introduction - Whys in Daniel Important?	ix
Chapter 1 - Repeat and Expand	1
Chapter 2 - God's Country	5
Chapter 3 - Daniel 11	11
Chapter 4 - Pagan Rome	17
Chapter 5 - Seventy Weeks of Probation	21
Chapter 6 - Who Is Israel?	29
Chapter 7 - Rome and the Holy Covenant	37
Chapter 8 - Rome Changes Garbs	41
Chapter 9 - The Time of the End	51
Chapter 10 - The Glorious Land	55
Chapter 11 - Tidings Out of the East	65
Chapter 12 - Michael Stands Up	71
Chapter 13 - "Shut up the Words"	77
Chapter 14 - The Latter Rain	83
Chapter 15 - Eleventh Hour Christians	91
Chapter 16 - The Missing Link	97

Introduction
Why is Daniel Important?

Is there a missing link, a piece of a message that will connect the past to the present and the future. There must be. Otherwise, why are we still here on this sinful earth, when we should have been in the heavenly Promised Land long ago? What is this missing link, and how will we know when we find it? Is it the tidings out of the east?

Are we being deceived? We need to understand that to bring about his deceptions, Satan will try to use the same end-time prophecies that we use. If we're only surface readers, we'll likely be turned in the wrong direction. We need to know the truths of God for ourselves. We really don't want to leave our understanding of last day events in the hands of others.

One of Satan's tricks is to place an act of history in our minds that will never happen. This is true in the case of the rapture. Most of Christendom today is waiting for an event that won't happen, the secret and unannounced visit of Christ to this earth, the rapture. According to the rapture teachers, believers will be swept away, here one second and gone the next.

Since it's not within the scope of this book to deal with the rapture, we won't be going there.[1] However, it's important to know that the same tricks the deceiver uses with the rapture could also be used here in Daniel 11.

When Bible students pick up a book that describes Daniel 11, many go directly to Daniel 11:40. They want to know who the two kings are that seem to be opponents in the last great battle on earth, at the "time of the end." One of these kings is from the north and the other from the south. Many take Daniel 11:40 as the primary focal text of Daniel 11. Of course, we need to know who these kings are and about this final conflict, so I agree this verse is very important. However, I consider it the second most important verse of focus. I choose verse 44 as the primary focal text of Daniel 11. Within verse 44 we can find the name of this book, *Tidings Out of the East*. What are these tidings and what will they do? Why from the east and north? Read on.

Daniel 11:40, Kings of the North and South

In the case of Daniel 11, books have been written that teach the king of the north to be Turkey, or the Papacy or Russia. We also need to find out who the king of the south is; does this refer to Egypt, China, Atheism or something else? The most recent popular belief is that it refers to Islam.

Why do we need to know for sure who the kings of the north and south are? Simply this, we could wait for a war or conflict to take place with Islam or China, only to wait for an event that never comes. Exactly who the kings of the north and south are, will appear later when we deal with our secondary focus text, Daniel 11:40. We will need to know to whom that verse applies.

Reading the News into the Text

We must be careful. If we interpret prophecy using the newspapers, we could err in trying to place today's news into a text where it doesn't belong. The correct method to interpret prophecy is to look at the prophecy itself, not reading into it recent headlines. The rest of Daniel and the book of Revelation were written for us to reach a proper understanding of the verses below. We will be referring to parts of these two prophetic books, but not covering them to the extent they should be understood. A wider knowledge of the Bible and a study outside of this book is necessary.

If I took all the books and manuscripts I have on the book of Daniel and put them in a pile on my desk, it would be about eighteen inches high and comprise about fifteen books. To read them all and filter out a totally accurate understanding would be very time consuming. The fact is, I have been reading them over the past forty years. I'm still not sure I correctly understand all the events noted in Daniel 10-12. However, having all the historical facts down to a no-fault basis is not necessary. What we need to get from these chapters in Daniel and in the Bible as a whole is what God wants us to get from them.

Our Secondary Text of Focus

Again, our secondary text of interest is Daniel 11:40. Although secondary to this author, it's primary to most students of Daniel. Here it is:

Why is Daniel Important? - Intro

"And at the time of the end shall the king of the south push at him: and the king of the north shall come against him like a whirlwind, with chariots, and with horsemen, and with many ships; and he shall enter into the countries, and shall overflow and pass over." Daniel 11:40.

Daniel's prophecies carry us through history from the time of Nebuchadnezzar, King of Babylon to the setting up of God's kingdom at the end of the world, a kingdom that will never be destroyed.

Paralleling Daniel in Revelation, God's eternal kingdom is set up with the seventh trumpet,

"And the seventh angel sounded; and there were great voices in heaven, saying, the kingdoms of this world are become [the kingdoms] of our Lord, and of his Christ; and he shall reign forever and ever." Rev. 11:15.

However, before Christ can be restored as a king, He must have a kingdom of believers. A kingdom without a king is not a kingdom. In the same vein, a kingdom without believers is also not a kingdom. Today, Jesus is our high priest, officiating in the most holy of the heavenly sanctuary, bearing our sins. He's not a king, because He hasn't received His kingdom yet. He'll receive it after it's restored with believers, but first the believers must be established. God's people must be restored to the image Adam had before the fall, because there will be no sin in the earth made new.

In Daniel 8:14 we are told the sanctuary will be restored to its original state, cleansed. Our primary text of focus, Daniel 11:44, the "tidings out of the east" has to do with God's people being restored; Daniel 11:44, "tidings out of the east," parallels both Daniel 8:14, "unto two-thousand three-hundred days, then shall the sanctuary be cleansed," and Daniel 7:10, "the judgment was set, and the books were opened."

Restoring the Kingdom

In Daniel 2, we read about the kingdom that will come to destroy all the earthly kingdoms before it. The kingdom was lost to Satan when he usurped it in Eden. Nevertheless, this kingdom will be restored to its Rightful King. It's the stone cut out without hands that Nebuchadnezzar saw in his dream,

"Thou saw till that a stone was cut out without hands, which smote the image upon his feet [that were] of iron and clay, and brake them to pieces. . . And in the days of these kings shall the God of heaven set up a kingdom, which shall never be destroyed: and the kingdom shall not be left to other people, [but] it shall break in pieces and consume all these kingdoms, and it shall stand for ever." Daniel 2:24, 44.

Tidings Out of the East

Daniel 7 tells us about the restoration of the King. The day Daniel saw this vision there was no king on the throne, ruling either in Judah or Samaria. Daniel 7 showed there would be no king to rule over God's people for many years; Babylon would rule first, then Persia, followed by Greece and Rome. After all that, a "little horn" would rule. These four great empires and the "little horn" must come and go before the king and kingdom will be restored. In the following text, Ezekiel informed the Jews that they will not have their True King until God sets up His King Jesus, "whose right it is" to be king,

"And thou, profane wicked prince of Israel, whose day is come, when iniquity [shall have] an end, Thus says the Lord GOD; Remove the diadem, and take off the crown: this [shall] not [be] the same: exalt [him that is] low, and abase [him that is] high. I will overturn, overturn, overturn, it: and it shall be no [more], until he come whose right it is; and I will give it [him]." Ezekiel 21:25-27.

Daniel said it this way,

"I saw in the night visions, and, behold, [one] like the Son of man came with the clouds of heaven, and came to the Ancient of days, and they brought him near before him. And there was given him dominion, and glory, and a kingdom, that all people, nations, and languages, should serve him: his dominion [is] an everlasting dominion, which shall not pass away, and his kingdom [that] which shall not be destroyed." Daniel 7:13, 14.

Restoring the Sanctuary

Daniel 8 speaks of the restoration of the sanctuary. It was through the sanctuary that God gave His plan of salvation to the Jews. Without the sanctuary, there was no hope for the people. God wanted to be with them, so He asked them to build the sanctuary. He said, ". . . let them make me a sanctuary; that I may dwell among them." Exodus 25:8. For the Jew, without the sanctuary, there was no salvation. It's still true today; we have a sanctuary in Heaven.

The restoration of the sanctuary is the theme of Daniel 8, in fact, all of Daniel. Daniel was hoping and looking forward to the restoration of the sanctuary and the city of Jerusalem. However, it sickened him to find that it was yet for "many days" far into the future. The sanctuary to be cleansed in Daniel 8:14 is at the end of time. Daniel asked a question that had an answer he wasn't looking for,

"And I heard, but I understood not: then said I, O my Lord, what [shall be] the end of these [things]? And he said, Go thy way, Daniel: for the words [are] closed up and sealed till the time of the end." Daniel 12:8, 9.

Why is Daniel Important? - Intro

Daniels visions are for our time. He wanted the kingdom restored. He wanted the King restored. He wanted the sanctuary restored to the kingdom, but he would have to wait. Nevertheless, he is to be heard and read again at the end of the world, the "time of the end." His words are for those living today. Everything will soon be restored.

Restoring the People

However, before the restoration of the kingdom, there is another necessary restoration, the restoration of the people. Sins are placed upon the sanctuary, but before the sanctuary can be cleansed, those who live therein by faith must stop sinning. They must stop polluting the sanctuary with their sins.

So, first the people must be restored, then the sanctuary, then the king with His kingdom. This is the theme of Daniel as well as the theme of Revelation. It's the theme of the entire Bible and the plan of salvation. We must have restoration.

We also need to remember that Daniel is a book of judgment. The name Daniel means, "God is Judge" or "God will Judge." Before the King, kingdom and sanctuary can be restored, the people of God must be judged. It's the judgment that restores; the judgment is very good news.

When telling Israel what God would do on the Day of Atonement, on the Day of Judgment, Moses wrote this good news blessing,

> "For on that day shall [the priest] make an atonement for you, to cleanse you, [that] ye may be clean from all your sins before the LORD."
> "And he shall make an atonement for the holy sanctuary, and he shall make an atonement for the tabernacle of the congregation, and for the altar, and he shall make an atonement for the priests, and for all the people of the congregation." Leviticus 16:30, 33.

The atonement was for the people, not the sanctuary alone. The final atonement, the cleansing of the sanctuary of Daniel 8:14 is an event for the people of God in the last days.

---

[1] A very good book that deals with the fallacy of the rapture is by Steve Wohlberg, *End Time Delusions*.

Chapter 1
Repeat and Expand Parallelism

Before we go into Daniel 10-12, we need to shortly review Daniel 2, 7, 8 and 9 and see how Bible prophecy uses the repeat and expand key throughout Daniel and Revelation. This device gives a condensed, skeletal view of history at first, then repeats it and expands on it. For example, Daniel 2 and the great image is a condensed view of history from the time of Nebuchadnezzar of Babylon to the end of the world.

The dream the king saw in Daniel 2 was of a man made up of different metals, gold, silver, brass and iron. We know that history has produced four main world empires, Babylon, Medo-Persia, Greece and Rome. Daniel declared Babylon as the head of gold. We're now in the feet, with no worldwide power in control. At the end of the world, as represented by the rock cut out "without hands" in Daniel 2, God will set up a kingdom that will never be destroyed.

Daniel 7 Repeats and Expands Daniel 2

Daniel 7 repeats these same four world empires and expands on them by telling us there would be a "little horn" that would supersede the others. Instead of using the parts of a man's body, as in Daniel 2, these four empires were represented by beasts. The lion was Babylon, the ram, Medo-Persia, the goat, Greece, all followed by a most terrible beast. Looking at history, we find this last beast to be Rome.

Although the first four kingdoms are represented by beasts of prey, the "little horn" is not. Instead, it came up out of the fourth beast, Rome. This "little horn" continues until the judgment at the end of the world. "But the judgment shall sit, and they shall take away his dominion, to consume and to destroy [it] unto the end." Daniel 7:26. Daniel 7 deals with this false king, the "little horn." Nevertheless, in the end, God will restore His kingdom with a restored king.

Tidings Out of the East

Much more could be quoted from Daniel 7, but since we're studying primarily Daniel 10-12, we won't spend much time on the rest of Daniel 7. However, a good knowledge of the previous chapters, Daniel 1-9, is essential to the understanding of 10-12. Daniel 10-12 expands greatly on the earlier visions of world history starting from Persia, continuing to the "time of the end," which is spoken of in our secondary verse of focus, Daniel 11:40.

Daniel 8

Daniel 8 repeats and expands on the previous chapters, paralleling the judgment in 7:26 with the cleansing of the sanctuary in 8:14. Daniel 8 tells of the restoration of the sanctuary, or temple of God. Please notice that the "little horn" of Daniel 7 and the "little horn" of Daniel 8 rule for quite some time, in fact, in Daniel 7 for 1260 years, "a time and times and the dividing of time." Daniel 7:25. After that, the judgment would come.

The vision of Daniel 8;14 continued for 2300 years, ending with the cleansing of the sanctuary. It reads, ". . . the sanctuary shall be cleansed." This can also be read, ". . . the sanctuary shall be restored to its rightful state." RSV. Remember, Daniel is about judgment and restoration of the sanctuary, a restoration of the people, and of the kingdom and the king.

The Same Little Horn

Some people teach that the little horn of Daniel 7 and Daniel 8 are different. However, using the *repeat and expand* method of prophetic interpretation, it's hard to see other than that they are the same. The little horn in Daniel 7 comes at the same time in history as the little horn of Daniel 8. To make the little horn two separate beings is complicated and confusing. [1]

For a chart on the comparison of Daniel 7 and 8, see the chart on the next page. When we begin our study of Daniel 10, 11 and 12, we will see how these chapters also parallel chapters 2, 7, 8 and John's book of Revelation. In Revelation also, the seven churches, the seven seals, and the seven trumpets all repeat and expand. The two prophetic books of Daniel and Revelation go hand in hand and parallel each other, telling the same history and prophetic future events connected with the "time of the end."

Not all the events mentioned in one chapter are repeated in the others, but the way the events are interwoven reveals to us the overall picture. God has not made it impossible to decode, but He wants His people to study and understand. "Many shall be purified, and made white, and tried; but the wicked shall do wickedly: and none of the wicked shall understand; but the wise shall understand." Daniel 12:10.

Parallels in Daniel 7 and 8

Daniel 7		Daniel 8	
Babylon, Lion	v.4		
Persia, Bear	v.5	Persia, Ram	v.3,20
Greece, Leopard	v.6	Greece, He-goat	v.5,21
Four heads	v.6	Four Winds, Great horn broken toward four winds	v.8
Pagan Rome, terrible beast	v.7, v.11,19,20	Pagan Rome Trampled on the host	v.9 v.10
Christian Rome, little horn	v.8	Christian Rome, the little horn.	
Change times and laws		"Daily" taken away. Sanctuary cast down. Trampled the host. Cast the truth to the ground.	v.11
Three and a half times	v.25	End of the time appointed Becomes mighty Destroys wonderfully	v.19 v.24 v.24
Wears out the saints	v.25	Destroys holy people Causes craft to prosper	v.25 v.25
Speaks words against God Dominion taken away Consumed in the end	v.25 v.11,26		

 Since the scope of this book is to stay with Daniel 10-12 as much as possible, not all that can be said, will be said. If the reader isn't familiar with Daniel 2-7, the easy-to-read Kindle book, *Bible Prophecy and Globalism* by this same author is recommended.
 It might be a good idea at this time to review Daniel 7 and 8. Check the parallelism shown in the chart above. One thing you will soon notice is that Babylon is found in Daniel 7 but not in Daniel 8. This is because Babylon was off the scene when the vision of Daniel 8

Tidings Out of the East

was given. At that time, Babylon had been replaced by the Persian Empire.

You might also notice that Pagan Rome is represented in Daniel 7 as a "terrible beast', but by no beast in Daniel 8. Rome is represented within one of the "four winds," the four directions, the four divisions of the Greek Empire. It took many years, but Rome gained power and territory as it took over all four directions, represented by the four Greek generals. Rome eventually took control of all the nations of the four corners of the earth, the four winds, but was itself from the north.

To come through Palestine, an army had to come from the north or south, because the sea was to the west and the desert to the east. Here in Daniel 8, God is initially establishing the two kings that will be of importance at the "time of the end," The kings of the north and south. This will lead up to our secondary verse of focus, Daniel 11:40.

"And at the time of the end shall the king of the south push at him: and the king of the north shall come against him like a whirlwind, with chariots, and with horsemen, and with many ships; and he shall enter into the countries, and shall overflow and pass over." Daniel 11:40.

Remember, our primary verse of focus is Daniel 11:44.

"But tidings out of the east and out of the north shall trouble him: therefore he shall go forth with great fury to destroy, and utterly to make away many." Daniel 11:44.

We'll have more on this later.

---

[1] For a more complete review of this two little horn's issue, see *Restoring the Holy of Holies - Revelation - A Seven-act Play*.

Chapter 2
God's Country

If we want to take the time to study them, the first visions of Daniel 2, 7, 8 and 9 are not difficult to follow. However, even though they have had an interpretation for hundreds of years, not everyone agrees how to interpret parts of them. On the other hand, Daniel 10, 11 and 12 are not so often dealt with nor understood, as they should be. However, it's important to note that God didn't inspire Daniel to write his book and not have it understood. Now is the time for Daniel's book to be read and understood because this is the "time of the end", we need to know what God has for us to learn in Daniel 10-12.

Keys open doors and prophetic keys open up past, present and future history. One key we need to understand is the history and prophetic future presented in the last three chapters of Daniel. We must know where Daniel was in his mind when he saw these prophecies. Within Daniel 11 and 12, we find kings mentioned, one from each of the four corners of the earth, but the kings of the north and south are the most important and the focal point of many expositors. Who are these two kings that fight with each other at the end of the world? Here again is the text.

"And at the time of the end shall the king of the south push at him: and the king of the north shall come against him like a whirlwind, with chariots, and with horsemen, and with many ships; and he shall enter into the countries, and shall overflow and pass over." Daniel 11:40.

You will find interpretations today that place China as the king of the south, others say it's Islam. Neither of these ideas have been popular in the past. As mentioned before, we must be careful not to interpret prophecy by the newspapers and TV news. We must let the Bible explain.

If I said the snow would come up from the south, you would probably question snow coming from that direction. Nevertheless, if you live in Australia, the farther south you go, the colder it gets. When we talk about the king of the north, we need to know where we, God's people, are in relationship to these two directions. What's north of us, and what's south. It's imperative we establish a point of reference. I'd like to suggest it's Palestine. This is where the kingdom, the king, and the sanctuary were located, along with God's people, all of which need to be restored. In the end, when all is restored, God's people will live in New Jerusalem on Mount Zion.

The 144,000 in Revelation 14 are seen on Zion. When New Jerusalem comes down, it will settle on the Mount of Olives.[1] If the reference point in these chapters is not Palestine, then where else could it be? If God's people are in Palestine, then who is to the north and who to the south?   With Jerusalem and the land of Israel as the focal point, we will begin our verse-by-verse interpretation of the last three chapters of Daniel, the restoration of the people of God, the kingdom and the king.

Daniel in Persia

10:1 In the third year of Cyrus king of Persia a thing was revealed unto Daniel, whose name was called Belteshazzar; and the thing [was] true, but the time appointed [was] long: and he understood the thing, and had understanding of the vision.

This was the year 534 B.C., when Cyrus the Great was King of the empire that ruled the world, including the land of Palestine where God's people lived. In 534 B.C., the third year of Cyrus, he decreed that the Jews could return to their homeland.

The words "time appointed"[2] are translated from a Hebrew word that means "warfare" or "conflict" The RSV translates it, "It was a great conflict." Ellen White tells us Daniel was given the view of a "mighty struggle."

"Through the prophet Daniel we are given a glimpse of this mighty struggle between the forces of good and the forces of evil.

"For <u>three weeks</u> Gabriel wrestled with the powers of darkness, seeking to counteract the influences at work on the mind of Cyrus; and before the contest closed, Christ Himself came to Gabriel's aid.' The prince of the kingdom of Persia withstood me <u>one and twenty days</u>,' Gabriel declares; 'but, lo, Michael, one of the chief princes, came to help me; and I remained there with the kings of Persia.' The highest agencies of heaven were working on the hearts of kings, and it was for the people of God to labor with the utmost activity to carry out the decree of Cyrus." *Patriarchs and Prophets*, p. 571, 2. Underlining supplied.

This warfare was not between two nations but between the powers of good and evil. God wanted to establish His people back to the land of Palestine from where they had been taken captive by Babylon. Daniel understood the conflict, "the thing." He was concerned about his people and mourned "one and twenty days."

10:2 In those days I Daniel was mourning three full weeks.

The answer to Daniel's prayer comes in verses 12 and 13 below. But, before that, he fasted "three full weeks."

10:3 I ate no pleasant bread, neither came flesh nor wine in my mouth, neither did I anoint myself at all, till three whole weeks were fulfilled.

It was Christ that appeared to Daniel while he was fasting on the bank of the Tigris River. From Christ Daniel received a vision. Later, Gabriel came and picked him up from the ground.

10:4 And in the four and twentieth day of the first month, as I was by the side of the great river, which [is] Hiddekel; [Tigris]

10:5 Then I lifted up mine eyes, and looked, and behold a certain man clothed in linen, whose loins [were] girded with fine gold of Uphaz:

10:6 His body also [was] like the beryl, and his face as the appearance of lightning, and his eyes as lamps of fire, and his arms and his feet like in colour to polished brass, and the voice of his words like the voice of a multitude.

10:7 And I Daniel alone saw the vision: for the men that were with me saw not the vision; but a great quaking fell upon them, so that they fled to hide themselves.

10:8 Therefore I was left alone, and saw this great vision, and there remained no strength in me: for my comeliness was turned in me into corruption, and I retained no strength.

10:9 Yet heard I the voice of his words: and when I heard the voice of his words, then was I in a deep sleep on my face, and my face toward the ground.

Tidings Out of the East

Daniel's friends "fled to hide themselves," for the glory of the Lord was before them, the Holy One of Israel. They couldn't withstand His glory. Even Daniel "retained no strength," and when I [Daniel] heard the voice of his words, then was I [Daniel] in a deep sleep on my face, and my face toward the ground." This couldn't have been an angel, for John was told in Revelation not to worship an angel.[3] Daniel saw Jesus and the vision, but it was Gabriel that picked him up.

Then Gabriel Came

10:10 And, behold, an hand touched me, which set me upon my knees and [upon] the palms of my hands.

10:11 And he said unto me, O Daniel, a man greatly beloved, understand the words that I speak unto thee, and stand upright: for unto thee am I now sent. And when he had spoken this word unto me, I stood trembling.

10:12 Then said he [Gabriel] unto me, Fear not, Daniel: for from the first day that thou didst set thine heart to understand, and to chasten thyself before thy God, thy words were heard, and I am come for thy words.

10:13 But the prince of the kingdom of Persia withstood me one and twenty days: [the three weeks of 10:2] but, lo, Michael, [Jesus] one of the chief princes, came to help me; and I remained there with the kings of Persia.

Ellen White Comments

"While Satan was striving to influence the highest powers in the kingdom of Medo-Persia to show disfavor to God's people, angels worked in behalf of the exiles. The controversy was one in which all heaven was interested. Through the prophet Daniel we are given a glimpse of this mighty struggle between the forces of good and the forces of evil. For three weeks Gabriel wrestled with the powers of darkness, seeking to counteract the influences at work on the mind of Cyrus; and before the contest closed, Christ Himself came to Gabriel's aid. "The prince of the kingdom of Persia withstood me one and twenty days," Gabriel declares; "but, lo, Michael, one of the chief princes, came to help me; and I remained there with the kings of Persia." Daniel 10:13. All that heaven could do in behalf of the people of God was done. The victory was finally gained; the forces of the enemy were held in check all the days of Cyrus, and all the days of his son Cambyses, who reigned about seven and a half years." *Prophets and Kings*, 571, 572.

10:14 Now I am come to make thee understand what shall befall thy people in the latter days: for yet the vision [is] for [many] days.

Gabriel was there, talking to Daniel and telling him about the end of time, the end of all things, "many days" "in the "latter days." Then, Jesus returns to Daniel.

10:15 And when he had spoken such words unto me, I set my face toward the ground, and I became dumb.

Jesus Returns

10:16 And, behold, [one] like the similitude of the sons of men touched my lips: then I opened my mouth, and spoke, and said unto him that stood before me, O my lord, by the vision my sorrows are turned upon me, and I have retained no strength.
10:17 For how can the servant of this my lord talk with this my lord? for as for me, straightway there remained no strength in me, neither is there breath left in me.
10:18 Then there came again and touched me [one] like the appearance of a man, and he strengthened me,
10:19 And said, O man greatly beloved, fear not: peace [be] unto thee, be strong, yea, be strong. And when he had spoken unto me, I was strengthened, and said, Let my lord speak; for thou hast strengthened me.

As in Daniel 2, 7, and 8, we see here also that the kingdom of Greece follows Persia as a world power.

10:20 Then said he, Knowest thou wherefore I come unto thee? and now will I return to fight with the prince of Persia: and when I am gone forth, lo, the prince of Greece shall come.
10:21 But I will show thee that which is noted in the scripture of truth: and [there is] none that holds with me in these things, but Michael your prince.

So ends Daniel 10, but not the episode of Daniel with the angel Gabriel. The story continues in Daniel 11.

---

[1] Zechariah 14:4.

[2] This "time appointed" is not to be confused with the "time appointed" in Daniel 8:19, 11:27, 29 or 35. Here in Daniel 10:1, the Strong's number is H6635, meaning warfare. In all the others it's H4150, meaning a special appointed time.

[3] See Revelation 22:8, 9.

Chapter 3
Daniel 11

Daniel 11 is really a continuation of chapter 10. There are no chapter separations in the original text. When this chapter opens, Daniel is still in Persia, however in the timeline of history, Greece is not far off. Daniel 11 takes us to the end of the world, "At the time of the end" and the two kings, from the north and the south. This is our secondary text of focus, Daniel 11:40. Once again, here is that text:

> "And at the time of the end shall the king of the south push at him: and the king of the north shall come against him like a whirlwind, with chariots, and with horsemen, and with many ships; and he shall enter into the countries, and shall overflow and pass over." Daniel 11:40.

There's a lot of history between verse 11:1 and 11:40. It takes a lot of time and effort to learn the historical events that apply to this chapter. Fortunately, others have done most of the research for us. In this book, I will try to give enough detail to convince but not too much to bore.[1]

Daniel 11 starts us in Persia.

11:1 Also I in the first year of Darius the Mede, [even] I, stood to confirm and to strengthen him.

Ellen White tells us: "The reign of Darius was honored of God. To him was sent the angel Gabriel, "to confirm and to strengthen him." *Patriarchs and Prophets*, 556.

11:2 And now will I show thee the truth. Behold, there shall stand up yet three kings in Persia; and the fourth shall be far richer than [they] all: and by his strength through his riches he shall stir up all against the realm of Grecia.

Tidings Out of the East

The Four Kings to Follow Cyrus
Cambyses	530-522 B.C.
Smerdis	522 B.C.
Darius the Great	522-486 B.C.
Xerxes	486-475 B.C.

11:3 And a mighty king shall stand up, that shall rule with great dominion, and do according to his will.

The first and mightiest of all the kings of Greece was Alexander the Great. In fact, he was the only king that had sole rule of Greece. His successors were four. When Alexander was strongest, after declaring himself a god, "when he shall stand up," he died. Alexander mentioned here in Daniel 11 corresponds to Daniel 8, where it says: "And the rough goat [is] the king of Greece: and the great horn that [is] between his eyes [is] the first king." Daniel 8:21.

His kingdom was divided into four:

11:4 And when he shall stand up, his kingdom shall be broken, and shall be divided toward the four winds of heaven; and not to his posterity, nor according to his dominion which he ruled: for his kingdom shall be plucked up, even for others beside those.

The kingdom wasn't given to his offspring, but divided among his four generals, Lysimachus in Thrace, Seleusus in Syria, Ptolemy in Egypt to the south of Palestine and Cassander in Macedonia to the north and west of the holy land.

11:5 And the king of the south shall be strong, and [one] of his princes; and he shall be strong above him, and have dominion; his dominion [shall be] a great dominion.

Prophecy here shifts us to two of the generals and their kingdoms, the kings of the north and south. This is because God's people were passively involved in the politics and wars of these two for the next few hundred years. They stood at the crossroads between the two, one to the north and one to the south. God mentions these two because He is interested in the welfare of His people, not in the affairs of any other power that's not involved in some way with Palestine and its inhabitants.

Ptolemy, based in Egypt, had a strong kingdom that extended through the land of Israel to the north up to Syria. Seleusus had a kingdom that stretched even farther, through Asia Minor, now Turkey, and upward and eastward to the river Indus.

11:6 And in the end of years they shall join themselves together; for the king's daughter of the south shall come to the king of the north to make an agreement: but she shall not retain the power of the arm; neither shall he stand, nor his arm: but she shall be given up, and they that brought her, and he that begat her, and he that strengthened her in [these] times.

As mentioned earlier, the kings of the north and south are mentioned repeatedly in Daniel 11. Syria was the king of the east when considering the kingdom of Greece breaking up to form four kingdoms from the four directions in reference to Greece. However, Syria lay north of Jerusalem and the Holy Land, so Syria is the king of the north in reference to God's people at this time. As armies conquer lands and set up new kingdoms, the king of the north will change, but will still be to the north, entering the Holy Land from the north.

Daniel 11:6-15 are a description of the wars between Syria to the north and Egypt to the south. Palestine was at the crossroads of these two nations and had to be passed through "passed over" to get to the opposing nations. The Great Sea was on the west and the desert was on the east. Invading armies from any direction other than south had to come from the north.

After many years of conflict, the two nations tried to work out a peace plan, "for the king's daughter of the south shall come to the king of the north to make an agreement." This daughter was Berenice, daughter of Ptolemy II of Egypt. The history of Berenice can easily be found elsewhere, so let's move on.

11:7 But out of a branch of her [Berenice] roots shall [one] stand up in his estate, which shall come with an army, and shall enter into the fortress of the king of the north, and shall deal against them, and shall prevail:

To avenge the murder of Berenice, her brother, Ptolemy III, "a branch of her roots," king of the south, waged war with Seleusus, king of the north. He was successful, overrunning Mesopotamia and Babylon to the north and east.

11:8 And shall also carry captives into Egypt their gods, with their princes, [and] with their precious vessels of silver and of gold; and he shall continue [more] years than the king of the north.

Tidings Out of the East

The RSV translates the KJV's rendering of, "and he shall continue [more] years than the king of the north," to "And for some years he shall refrain from attacking the king of the north."

11:9 So the king of the south shall come into [his] kingdom, and shall return into his own land.

This seems to be repeating the previous verse. However, if we use the RSV, we read, "Then the latter [king of the north] shall come into the realm of the king of the south, but shall return into his own land." Seleusus attacked Egypt but was repelled. He then returned "into his own land."

11:10 But his sons shall be stirred up, and shall assemble a multitude of great forces: and [one] shall certainly come, and overflow, and pass through: then shall he return, and be stirred up, [even] to his fortress.

The two sons of Seleusus vowed to revenge their father and get back all the territory lost in the previous war. Again, the king of the north, Antiochus III Magnus attacked Egypt in 218 B.C.
"And [one] shall certainly come, and overflow, and pass through." It was Antiochus alone; his brother had died before the conflict. The battle was in Palestine. He would "come" to Palestine, "overflow" the Holy Land, and "pass through." Palestine was now in the hands of the north.
Remember, Daniel and the visions are in reference to Palestine, to come together in battle, the kings of the north and south had to pass through or "overflow" the land of God's people.

11:11 And the king of the south shall be moved with choler, and shall come forth and fight with him, [even] with the king of the north: and he shall set forth a great multitude; but the multitude shall be given into his hand.

Ptolemy IV Philopater from the south came at Antiochus Magnus in the north with an army of 60,000 "a great multitude." Magnus had 70,000, but was defeated in the Battle of Gaza in B.C.217. Palestine once more changed hands. The "multitude" (14,000 of the 60,000) of the king of the north was given "into the hand" of the king of the south. The south was clearly the victor.

11:12 [And] when he hath taken away the multitude, his heart shall be lifted up; and he shall cast down [many] ten thousands: but he shall not be strengthened [by it].

Ptolemy was so overjoyed with his victory that he personally led a victory march into Jerusalem. Feeling so proud and confident, "his heart was lifted up," he offered sacrifices at the temple in Jerusalem.

History has recorded that he also tried to enter the most holy place of God's temple in spite of protests. "He was smitten from God with such a terror and confusion of mind that he was carried out of the place in a manner half dead." This angered him so much that he had as many as 40,000 Jews killed in B.C.213. In this way, he "cast down many." Instead of being "strengthened by it," the king died at the young age of thirty-seven. He was succeeded by his five-year-old son, Ptolemy V Epiphanes.

11:13 For the king of the north shall return, and shall set forth a multitude greater than the former, and shall certainly come after certain years with a great army and with much riches.

Again, the king of the north, Antiochus Magnus, came against Egypt and Ptolemy V, the child king. He invaded Palestine near Jordan, defeating the Egyptians and retaking Judea.

11:14 And in those times there shall many stand up against the king of the south: also the robbers of thy people shall exalt themselves to establish the vision; but they shall fall.

Others tried to overtake the king of the south, including the Syrians, the king of Macedonia, Rome and even the Egyptians themselves who hated the rule over them by the Greeks of the Ptolemy dynasty. But, who are the "robbers of thy people?" What is the "vision?"

The American Standard Version (ASV) translates "robbers of thy people" as "the violent among the people." The RSV has it, "The men of violence among thy people." This is because the Hebrew word translated in the KJV, "robbers," should be translated "sons of violence."

It could then be translated "violence against thy people" or "the men of violence among thy people." The second is preferred because only those among God's people could "establish the vision." The vision was that of Daniel 8 and 9, the 2300 years and the 490 years embedded within the 2300.

Tidings Out of the East

Antiochus Epiphanes

The vision is the vision of the 2300 days. Many even today still try to tie the end of the 2300 days to Antiochus Epiphanes who desecrated the temple by offering a swine on it. The restoration or cleansing of the temple (sanctuary) at that time was thought to be the fulfillment of the 2300 days with Antiochus being the "little horn" of Daniel 8. They saw the 2300 days as literal days, not years. As days, they would then end in the time of Antiochus, in those days, not in 1844. By trying to make this the truth, the violent people among God's people worked to "establish the vision," using the Maccabean Wars. Of course that was not the true fulfillment, so "they shall fall;" that is to say, those who used violence failed.

We will deal with how God's people could "establish the vision." later in chapter 5.

11:15 So the king of the north shall come, and cast up a mount, and take the most fenced cities: and the arms of the south shall not withstand, neither his chosen people, neither [shall there be any] strength to withstand.

At this time, the Seleucid Empire of the north failed and was annexed by Rome. Rome eventually took over Egypt to the south and became the new king of the north, eventually, world ruler over both north and south. However, since its capital and namesake was to the north and west, it became the new king of the north as far as Daniel and the Holy Land is concerned.

---

[1] See A.T. Jones in *Empires of Prophecy*.

Chapter 4
Pagan Rome

In the timeline of world history, Rome comes after Greece. We can see this by not only reading the history books, but also by following the parallelism of the earlier visions of Daniel 2, 7 and 8. The following verses of Daniel 11 especially parallel the same event of Daniel 8. Continuing in Daniel 11, we read,

11:16 But he that cometh against him shall do according to his own will, and none shall stand before him: and he shall stand in the glorious land, which by his hand shall be consumed.

In 168 B.C. at the Battle of Pydna, Rome defeated Phillip of Macedon, removing the last of the opposition north of Palestine. Rome's ambassador then ordered Antiochus Epiphanes out of Egypt to the south, establishing a universal dominion, securing rule of the north and south over Palestine, standing in "the glorious land."

The RSV translates what the KJV reads, "which by his hand shall be consumed", as, "And all of it [universal dominion] shall be in his power." Rome was now in charge.

11:17 He shall also set his face to enter with the strength of his whole kingdom, and upright ones with him; thus shall he do: and he shall give him the daughter of women, corrupting her: but she shall not stand [on his side], neither be for him.

In Daniel 11:6, the same Hebrew word translated there as "an agreement" is translated here as "upright ones." The translation of "agreement" works better, because in B.C.161, the Jews made "an agreement" of friendship with the Romans. Unfortunately, this showed their faith in man rather than in God.

Tidings Out of the East

The phrase, "Daughter of Women" is often thought to be Cleopatra, but how did Rome corrupt her? More likely, this refers to the Children of God as represented by a woman. "I have likened the daughter of Zion to a comely and delicate [woman]." Jeremiah 6:2. Song of Solomon calls Israel, "the daughter of Zion," or "the daughter of my people." Then too, if Jesus is the Son of Man, could His church, His people, then be the daughter of women?

Think on this, God is more interested in His people than a princess of the southern part of the kingdom, in spite of the fact historians are more interested in Cleopatra. Israel was corrupted when she made an alliance with a heathen nation, which was forbidden as far back as Moses. Instead of making flesh their arm, they should have put their faith in God.

This "daughter of women", God's people, lived with the Romans and worked with them, yet demanded and received a certain amount of self-rule. The Jewish Sanhedrin existed and ruled in Christ's time, but with limited powers. The Jews were neither "on his side," Caesar's, representing the Romans, nor were they "for him."

11:18 After this shall he turn his face unto the isles, and shall take many: but a prince for his own behalf shall cause the reproach offered by him to cease; without his own reproach he shall cause [it] to turn upon him.

The "isles" are the outlying countries, beyond the lands controlled by the Romans. The Romans warred to extend their territory, even as far as France and England.

Julius Caesar was a great, victorious general of these campaigns, and he took over the control of Rome as a Caesar, setting himself up as an absolute ruler, disregarding the democratic process. He did this on his "own behalf." Having a king or absolute ruler is a "reproach", a disgrace or a shame to the democratic form of government. Yet, the Senate praised and honored Julius to the point where he was given powers beyond the principles of democracy. He was later killed by Senate members.

11:19 Then he shall turn his face toward the fort of his own land: but he shall stumble and fall, and not be found.

Pagan Rome - 4

After Julius Caesar's foreign conquests, he returned to his own land to receive the honors of being dictator for life, commander-in-chief. He was proclaimed a holy man. Nevertheless, he was murdered by those in the Senate who hypocritically honored him. He "shall...not be found."

11:20 Then shall stand up in his estate a raiser of taxes [in] the glory of the kingdom: but within few days he shall be destroyed, neither in anger, nor in battle.

Caesar Augustus followed Julius, and we all should know him as the Caesar at the time of Jesus' birth. Every Christmas we hear these words, "And it came to pass in those days, that there went out a decree from Caesar Augustus, that all the world should be taxed." Luke 2:1.

"In the glory of the kingdom" refers to what is thought to be the golden age of Rome. However, it also could be referring to the honor the kingdom received because it was blessed at this time by the appearance of the Messiah, the birth of Jesus.

Augustus died in bed, peaceably at the age of seventy-six. Even today, to many, that seems like a long life, but in comparison to eternity, it's but a "few days." He died in A.D. 14, "neither in anger, nor in battle."

11:21 And in his estate shall stand up a vile person, to whom they shall not give the honour of the kingdom: but he shall come in peaceably, and obtain the kingdom by flatteries.

Tiberius followed and was one of Rome's greatest generals. However, he came to be remembered as a dark, reclusive, ruler. Pliny the Elder called him "the gloomiest of men." Because of this gloom and reluctance to serve as emperor, he wasn't given the "honor of the kingdom." He only ruled because his mother divorced his real father and married Augustus, his stepfather. Then, upon the death of Augustus, she procured the kingdom for her son "by flatteries".

11:22 And with the arms of a flood shall they be overflowed from before him, and shall be broken; yea, also the prince of the covenant.

Like most tyrants, Tiberius destroyed his enemies and all others who would be a threat to him, if necessary, even the Messiah. Many

Tidings Out of the East

thousands were killed by the emperor's suspicions, "with the arms of a flood." In addition, as most despots do, he paid informants throughout the kingdom, including anyone who would gladly turn Pilate in for being lenient with Jesus. The rulers of the Jews knew this and threatened Pilate by saying, "If you let this man [Prince of the Covenant] go, you are not Caesar's friend: whosoever makes himself a king speaks against Caesar." John 19:12. Although our sins killed Jesus in a legal sense, a Roman governor tried and condemned Him, had Him nailed to the cross and assigned Roman soldiers to stand guard over His body at the tomb.

Chapter 5
Seventy Weeks of Probation

Jesus the Messiah died in the year A.D.31. Three and a half years later, the 490 years of Daniel 9 ended in A.D.34. By the end of this period, the Jews were to have completed certain requirements. This was probationary time. In the next verse, we see what these conditions were and that it was indeed probationary time. Here are the requirements,

> "Seventy weeks are determined upon thy people and upon thy holy city, to finish the transgression, and to make an end of sins, and to make reconciliation for iniquity, and to bring in everlasting righteousness, and to seal up the vision and prophecy, and to anoint the most Holy." Daniel 9:24

Seventy weeks are Determined (decreed).

The Jews were in captivity, first in Babylon and later in Persia. They wanted to go back to their homeland in Palestine. They were exiled because of disobedience, but God was giving them a time to get things straightened out, to be exact, 490 years, reaching to the death of Messiah and shortly beyond to A.D. 34.

If the Jews had fulfilled the requirements and accepted their Messiah, we should expect they would have received great blessings. Up to that time, the nation of Israel was the literal nation based in the Holy Land. Would we expect it to be otherwise?

However, anyone on probation must meet certain requirements in order to remain in good standing. If not, then it's back to jail. The Jews, in a sense, were in jail, captives in another land with no king and no kingdom of their own. If they should fail to meet the requirements, what would be their consequences?

If they didn't obey as they should and fail to meet the obligations of their probation, who or where would Israel be? To whom would the

Old Testament promises to Israel belong? If God's chosen people didn't fulfill their destiny, who would take their place? Wouldn't God have to transfer all these promised blessings to another country or people? Who would this be?

As we well know, when the Jews made their last decision against Jesus and His resurrection, Paul and others were sent to the Gentiles. So then, are the chosen people of God from the Gentiles? Is so, the meaning of Israel would have to be changed, even spiritualized. That is to say, the nation of Israel, after literal Israel's final rejection, would have to be figurative rather than literal. Paul said it this way, "And if ye [be] Christ's, then are ye Abraham's seed, and heirs according to the promise." Galatians 3:29. In Paul's day and onward into the Christian era, a child of Abraham is not one born as a literal descendant of Abraham, but one who believes in and belongs to Christ.

By Faith

God had chosen Abraham as the first member of the nation of Israel, but the blessing would come only through his son Isaac. Isaac was the child of faith, and those that have faith are the only true children of Abraham, the sons of Isaac.

"Neither, because they are the seed of Abraham, [are they] all children: but, In Isaac shall thy seed be called. That is, they which are the children of the flesh, these [are] not the children of God: but the children of the promise are counted for the seed." Romans 9:7, 8.

It's not those who are born of Abraham according to the flesh, but those who are of Abraham and Isaac, according to the promise, according to faith. Paul makes it clear, "And if ye [be] Christ's, then are ye Abraham's seed, and heirs according to the promise." Galatians 3:29.

After the 490 years of probation in A.D.34, God had no more special blessing for literal Israel as a nation, because they, as a nation, rejected their Messiah, thereby breaking their probation. That leaves the new Israel a spiritual Israel, with a global existence, comprising members throughout the world. It was no longer a geopolitical country with its center in Jerusalem in the Middle East. Their new city was New Jerusalem, which is now in heaven, which will come down at the end of the millennium. Where else could it be, for the Jews failed to keep the conditions of this 490-year prophecy and rejected their Messiah. God could have chosen another nation, but He didn't. Instead, He sent the disciples out to the Gentile world to evangelize the world. Then, those that believed are the children of God, the sons of Israel, by faith. By faith, they're of Israel with their home in the New Jerusalem, which will be their final home after the millennium in the Promised Land of the new earth.

In the middle of the last week of the 490 years of Jewish probation, Messiah gave His life for all. The Jews had three and a half years after Jesus started His ministry to get things right, that is, to react correctly to His first advent. However, they failed both the three and a half years before His death as well as the three and a half years after it.

Let's look again in more detail at the conditions for their acceptance at the end of the 490 years? These are what was expected of them, and we can be sure there would be a consequence, if they failed. Unfortunately, they failed, so the message was sent to the Gentiles.

1: They were to finish the transgression.

The Jews didn't finish the transgression, but added to it by rejecting the Messiah. They had transgressed so often that God sent them into captivity, first to the Babylonians, then the Persians and Greeks, finally to the Romans in Christ's day.

2. They were to "make an end of sins."

I believe this to be an appositive, that is to say, it means the same as the sentence previous, "to finish the transgression." To make and end of sins is to finish the transgression.

3: They were to, "make reconciliation for iniquity."

For the word "reconciliation," Strong's gives these meanings, *cover, cancel, forgive* or *pardon*. This is justification, when our sins are covered, *cancelled, pardoned* and *forgiven,*. If the Jews had seen the death of Jesus for what it was, obeyed and preached it to all the nations, the Jewish nation and the world could have been reconciled, forgiven, justified. It was God's plan that the nation of Israel, the biological sons and daughters of Abraham would have been the blessed people behind the preaching of the Gospel. This was God's promise to Abraham, to make of him a great nation, to be a light to the Gentiles.

4. They were "to bring in everlasting righteousness."

This certainly didn't happen in the first century, but could have. This is sanctification. When we see Jesus on the cross for us, we're drawn to Him. From Him we receive forgiveness and the Holy Spirit for sanctification. Everlasting, total righteousness is a product of the final atonement, the cleansing of the sanctuary. Because the Jews failed in their probationary time, God's final cleansing was postponed many years, even to our time, to 1844 and beyond.

However, you might ask, if the Jews of Christ's day could have finished up the work as typified in the cleansing of the sanctuary, what about the end of the 2300 years and the other prophecies from the time of Christ to the end of the world, even to 1844. What do we do with those? The answer is next.

5: The Jews of the first century were "to seal up the vision and prophecy."

Strong's gives the number for "to seal up" as H2856. It's the Hebrew word "chatham," pronounced *khaw-tham*. It's defined as, "A primitive root; to *close* up; especially to *seal:* - make an end, mark, seal (up), stop."

The Jews had the chance to "seal up" or stop the vision of the 2300 days. It had to be that vision, because Daniel is not in vision here in Daniel 9; Gabriel is talking to him face to face, appearing to him while he was praying. It was the 2300-day vision of Daniel 8, the one Daniel had been praying about.

If the Jews had been faithful at the end of the 490 years, as God had asked of them, they would have "sealed up" the 2300-year prophecy. This is because the final atonement, the final cleansing would have soon taken place, likely even within the first century. The remaining days would not have been necessary. It's sad. They were not faithful, and the vision of the 2300 days couldn't be "sealed up." Therefore, the 2300 days must continue to 1844 and beyond.

Because the Jews failed in their calling, the prophecy remained open. It's now left for spiritual Israel to fulfill the new covenant promise, to be judged in the final atonement. It can't be fulfilled by the present-day geopolitical nation of Israel in the Middle East. As a nation, they had been chosen as a company entity. Therefore, for them to be the fulfillment of the promise, they would have to accept Jesus as their Messiah as a nation, a group made up of mostly believers. If we don't have a nation of mostly believers, then we cannot name the Israel of the Middle East the people of God.

As a result of their failure to keep the conditions of their probation, the descendants of Abraham, in the flesh, are only true Israelites as long as they believe in Christ. "And if ye [be] Christ's, then are ye Abraham's seed, and heirs according to the promise." Galatians 3:29.

Actually, that's the way it always has been. Only those of any century who can rightfully number themselves among true Israel have to accept Christ as the Messiah, before and after the day Jesus came in the flesh. In the Old Testament they looked forward to what Messiah would do, He would die as the Lamb of God. In the New Testament they look back at what He did, He died a lamb so that we can live.

More about who Israel is in the next chapter.

6: Lastly, the Jews of the first century were to "anoint the Most Holy."

This anointing is of Christ as king, not as the high priest. After His death and ascension, He was already anointed High Priest three and a half years before the end of the 490 years. On the other hand, Christ is anointed king after His work in the Holy of Holies is finished, after the people are without sin, fully righteous, not of themselves but in and through the power of the Holy Spirit living within.

Look Once Again At The Order.

1. They were to finish what had caused them to be in exile, the transgression.

2. They were to be justified and then sanctified.

3. The vision of the 2300 years was to be sealed up and discontinued, annulled. The final atonement would not come.

4. Finally, Jesus would be anointed king and come as the King of Kings and Lord of Lords.

Alas, that was not to happen. The Jews were rejected. Jerusalem was destroyed in A.D.70, and, as foretold in Deuteronomy 28, they were scattered among the nations. It need not have been. Ellen White tells us, "Had Israel as a nation preserved her allegiance to Heaven, Jerusalem would have stood forever, the elect of God. Jeremiah 17:21-25." *The Great Controversy*, p. 18.

Tidings Out of the East

The Blessings, if Faithful
Is it truly possible for the Jews to be rejected? Let's read from Deuteronomy 28. This chapter is often referred to as the "Blessing and the Curses."

No explanation should be necessary for the text below. The blessing and the curses are clear; they speak for themselves,

> "And it shall come to pass, if thou shalt hearken diligently unto the voice of the LORD thy God, to observe [and] to do all his commandments which I command thee this day, that the LORD thy God will set thee on high above all nations of the earth: And all these blessings shall come on thee, and overtake thee, if thou shalt hearken unto the voice of the LORD thy God. Blessed [shalt] thou [be] in the city, and blessed [shalt] thou [be] in the field. Blessed [shall be] the fruit of thy body, and the fruit of thy ground, and the fruit of thy cattle, the increase of thy kine, and the flocks of thy sheep. Blessed [shall be] thy basket and thy store. Blessed [shalt] thou [be] when thou comest in, and blessed [shalt] thou [be] when thou goest out." . . .And the LORD shall make thee the head, and not the tail; and thou shalt be above only, and thou shalt not be beneath; if that thou hearken unto the commandments of the LORD thy God, which I command thee this day, to observe and to do [them]: . . ." Deuteronomy 28:1-6, 13.

The Curses, if Unfaithful
> "But it shall come to pass, if thou wilt not hearken unto the voice of the LORD thy God, to observe to do all his commandments and his statutes which I command thee this day; that all these curses shall come upon thee, and overtake thee: Cursed [shalt] thou [be] in the city, and cursed [shalt] thou [be] in the field. Cursed [shall be] thy basket and thy store. Cursed [shall be] the fruit of thy body, and the fruit of thy land, the increase of thy kine, and the flocks of thy sheep. Cursed [shalt] thou [be] when thou comest in, and cursed [shalt] thou [be] when thou goest out. . . .The LORD shall bring thee, and thy king which thou shalt set over thee, unto a nation which neither thou nor thy fathers have known; and there shalt thou serve other gods, wood and stone. And thou shalt become an astonishment, a proverb, and a byword, among all nations whither the LORD shall lead thee." Deuteronomy 28:15-19, 36, 37.

The Destruction of Jerusalem
Interestingly, God not only told Israel that if they were unfaithful, they would be cursed, but added that a nation would cause them to do unspeakable things to themselves. In the following verse, we find the destruction of Jerusalem by a "far" country with a language they didn't know, "a tongue thou shalt not understand." It also predicts the eating of their own children, which took place in A.D.70 during the "siege" of Jerusalem. Then they would be scattered, He "shall scatter thee among all people."

Seventy Weeks of Probation - 5

"The LORD shall bring a nation against thee from far, from the end of the earth, [as swift] as the eagle flieth; a nation whose tongue thou shalt not understand; A nation of fierce countenance, which shall not regard the person of the old, nor show favour to the young: And he shall eat the fruit of thy cattle, and the fruit of thy land, until thou be destroyed: which [also] shall not leave thee [either] corn, wine, or oil, [or] the increase of thy kine, or flocks of thy sheep, until he have destroyed thee. And he shall besiege thee in all thy gates, until thy high and fenced walls come down, wherein thou trustedst, throughout all thy land: and he shall besiege thee in all thy gates throughout all thy land, which the LORD thy God hath given thee. And thou shalt eat the fruit of thine own body, the flesh of thy sons and of thy daughters, which the LORD thy God hath given thee, in the siege, and in the straitness, wherewith thine enemies shall distress thee:. . . So that he will not give to any of them of the flesh of his children whom he shall eat: because he hath nothing left him in the siege, and in the straitness, wherewith thine enemies shall distress thee in all thy gates. . . And the LORD shall scatter thee among all people, from the one end of the earth even unto the other; and there thou shalt serve other gods, which neither thou nor thy fathers have known, [even] wood and stone." Deuteronomy 28:49-53, 55, 64.   Emphasis supplied.

Oh! What could have been!

----

[1] Is Something New Here? What is being said here is this. If the Jews had done according to what was expected of them, soon after the end of the 490 years the final atonement would have been realized. Upon the conclusion of the Day of Atonement, Christ would have been anointed King, coming in the clouds of heaven. This could have all happened, possibly even within the first century. Nevertheless, they were not faithful, and the vision was not sealed up. It was left unsealed until 1844.

Is this a new idea? It is to me. Why this new idea? Recently, every time I read Daniel 9:24 about these conditions due at the end of the 490 years, I have wondered what would have happened if the Jews of Jesus' day had been faithful. In addition, when I read that the vision could be "sealed up," I have wondered what that could do to the vision, except to cancel it. Therefore, I am here proposing what is at least new to me. Possibly someone else has considered the same question at some time.

Chapter 6
Who is Israel?

Today, the popular teaching of the rapture has spread to many of the churches. It pinpoints the Israel in the modern day land of Palestine as the recipient of the blessing God has for His people in the last days. That is, all the blessings and promises of the Old Testament are now, in these last days, to be given to the geo-political nation of Israel, set up in Palestine in the late 1940's. However, is this the case? Who is a Jew today, and who is not?

The first Jew was Abraham, because God called him out of Babylon to set up his descendents in the land of Palestine. He chose Abraham because he believed. God promised to make of him a great nation, because he believed.

"Now the LORD had said unto Abram, Get out of thy country, and from thy kindred, and from thy father's house, unto a land that I will show thee: And I will make of thee a great nation, and I will bless thee, and make thy name great; and you will be a blessing:" Genesis 12:1, 2.

Abraham believed and is known as the father of the Jews, because he was the first Jew, called through faith. Yes, he believed, ". . .Abraham believed God, and it was counted unto him for righteousness." Romans 4:3. Can we expect to be saved because we are the physical seed of Abraham? If not, who will be saved? Who? Those that believe.

All Israel Shall be Saved
Who of Israel will be saved? Paul answers it this way,

"And so all Israel shall be saved: as it is written, There shall come out of Sion the Deliverer, and shall turn away ungodliness from Jacob:" Romans 11:26

Tidings Out of the East

That's good news, the gospel. Therefore, all we need to do is join with Israel, and we will be saved. Again, we ask, who is Israel? Paul tells us, ". . . For they [are] not all Israel, which are of Israel:" Romans 9:6. We see that it's possible to be in Israel but not of Israel. This can happen because we have two Israels, one is the literal Israel, a nation of people who are born of the flesh. They are children of Abraham in the flesh. The other Israel is a nation of believers who exercise faith, the children of faith. Paul tells us, "Neither, because they are the seed of Abraham, [are they] all children: but, In Isaac shall thy seed be called." Romans 9:7.

Abraham and the Promise

To understand this, we have to recall the story of Abraham, Ishmael and Isaac. God promised Abraham a son, but because he was very old and Sarah was past her ability to have children, Abraham attempted to work out God's promise by taking his wife's handmaid, Hagar, to conceive a child with her.

> "For it is written, that Abraham had two sons, the one by a bondmaid, the other by a freewoman. But he [who was] of the bondwoman was born after the flesh; but he of the freewoman [was] by promise. Which things are an allegory: for these are the two covenants; the one from the mount Sinai, which genders to bondage, which is Agar. For this <u>Agar is mount Sinai in Arabia,</u> and answers to Jerusalem which now is, and is in bondage with her children. But <u>Jerusalem which is above</u> is free, which is <u>the mother of us all</u>." Galatians 4:22-26.

Acting contrary to God's promise, this was Abraham's own "work" of fulfilling the promise. However, the promise of God was that Abraham should have the faith to believe in God's promise. Later God worked a miracle to keep His promise with Sarah, even though her womb was dead. Therefore, Isaac is the child of the promise, the child of faith, and "In Isaac shall thy seed be called." Romans 9:7.

Taking Hagar (Agar) to produce the promised seed is represented by Mount Sinai in Arabia. The Old Covenant was bondage to the law because the Israelites promised to keep it, but could not and did not. Their promise to keep the law was their promise, not God's promise.[1] Those in bondage to the law are now in old Jerusalem. On the other hand, those who are of the New Covenant are of the New Jerusalem, the heavenly city, "which is the mother of us all."

Those who are of the seed of Abraham are not all of the promise unless they live with the promise. What is that promise? It is the promise of a Deliverer.

> "And so <u>all Israel shall be saved</u>: as it is written, There shall come out of Sion the Deliverer, and shall turn away ungodliness from Jacob:" Romans 11:26

The "all Israel" that will be saved are those who accept the Deliverer who comes out of Zion. To be in spiritual Israel and be saved, we must accept the Messiah, Jesus Christ. "All Israel" will be saved because spiritual Israel will be made up only of those who are of faith and accept the Messiah. Because they have faith, they can and will be saved. Those who are not of faith in the life and work of the Messiah are not of Israel.

Let's look at Romans 9:6 again, this time with the two Israels defined, ". . . For they [are] not all Israel [Born of faith, having faith in the Promise] which are of Israel: [flesh born descendants of Abraham]" Romans 9:6. Jesus said to Nicodemus, "You must be born again." John 3:7. Those born in the blood line of Abraham still need to be born again of the Spirit. They must have a new life, not trusting in their physical birth, being a literal descendent of Abraham alone.

Paul tells us we must be believers in the Messiah, "And if ye [be] Christ's, then are ye Abraham's seed, and heirs according to the promise." Galatians 3:29. Rejecting Christ is rejecting the new birth. It's rejecting membership in the New Jerusalem, the spiritual nation of Israel.

We Must Believe in the Deliverer

In order to be part of "all Israel" and be saved, we must accept the Deliverer and be delivered. Otherwise, we might be in physical Israel, yet not in spiritual. The geo-political nation of Israel in the Middle East today has rejected their messiah, and although children of Abraham in the flesh, they are not his children by faith in the promise of God. Only if they choose to believe can they be in the Israel of the promise. They must accept Jesus the Christ.

If we expect the promises of the Old Testament concerning Israel to apply to the present day nation of Israel, then we should expect them to turn as a nation to the Messiah they have rejected thus far. They need to accept Him as a nation, because as a nation they were a theocracy, headed and controlled by God as their rightful king. The Jews today believe they are receiving the blessings because they are a part of the Jewish nation, therefore *as a nation* they must believe. It's sad, but that will never happen.

The nation of Israel having only some Christians, some Messiah believers among them, does not qualify them as anything other than the literal, born-of-the-flesh Israelites. Only those among them that belong to Christ belong to the Israel of the promise. Because the nation of Israel does not accept Christ as the Messiah, the nation of Israel is not the nation of Israel, except in the "flesh." What was true in the first century, Paul's time, is true today. "For they [are] not all Israel, which are of Israel," Roman 9:6.

It all started with Abraham, "Even as Abraham believed God, and it was accounted to him for righteousness." Galatians 3:6. It is those who have faith that are the children of Abraham. John the Baptist said to the Jews,

> ". . .O generation of vipers, who hath warned you to flee from the wrath to come? Bring forth therefore fruits meet for repentance: And think not to say within yourselves, We have Abraham to [our] father: for I say unto you, that God is able of these stones to raise up children unto Abraham. And now also the ax is laid unto the root of the trees: therefore every tree which brings not forth good fruit is hewn down, and cast into the fire." Matthew 3:7-10.

Two Nations of Israel

When Jesus spoke to the Pharisees in John 8, He was showing the two meanings of Israel, the one of the flesh and the other of the spirit. They claimed Abraham as their father, and truly they were sons of Abraham in the flesh. Nevertheless, they were not the children of Abraham, true Israelites in the spirit. If they had been, they would have done the works of Abraham,

> "They answered and said unto him, Abraham is our father. Jesus said unto them, If you were Abraham's children, you would do the works of Abraham. But now you seek to kill me, a man that has told you the truth, which I have heard of God: this did not Abraham.
> "You do the deeds of your father. Then said they to him, We be not born of fornication; we have one Father, [even] God. Jesus said unto them, If God were your Father, you would love me: for I proceeded forth and came from God; neither came I of myself, but he sent me. Why do ye not understand my speech? [even] because ye cannot hear my word." John 8:39-43

Speaking to the Jews, the children of Abraham in the flesh, Jesus said,

"Behold, thou art called a Jew, and rest in the law, and make your boast of God, And know [his] will, and approve the things that are more excellent, being instructed out of the law; And are confident that you thyself are a guide of the blind, a light of them which are in darkness, An instructor of the foolish, a teacher of babes, which has the form of knowledge and of the truth in the law. You therefore which teaches another, teach not yourself? You that preaches a man should not steal, do you steal? . . . You that make your boast of the law, through breaking the law do you dishonor God? For the name of God is blasphemed among the Gentiles through you, as it is written. For circumcision verily profits, if you keep the law: but if you be a breaker of the law, your circumcision is made uncircumcision. Therefore if the uncircumcision keep the righteousness of the law, shall not his uncircumcision be counted for circumcision?" Romans 2:17-26

God's Special Sign - Circumcision

The special sign the Jews were to carry with them in their bodies was circumcision. This was their indentifying mark, attesting to the fact they were Jews, the children of God. Circumcision was saying to the gentiles, "I belong to God, my Father." However, circumcision was to be a sign of obedience in faith, not merely a sign of fleshly birth. They were to be circumcised, showing obedience to the law in the spirit, not in obedience to the law "in the flesh." In other words, if they were circumcised according to the Law of Moses, they were circumcised only as stated in the law, "in the flesh." However, they needed to be also circumcised "of the heart", in the spirit.

"And shall not uncircumcision which is by nature, if it fulfills the law, judge you, who by the letter and circumcision does transgress the law? For he is not a Jew, which is one outwardly; neither [is that] circumcision, which is outward in the flesh: But he [is] a Jew, which is one inwardly; and circumcision [is that] of the heart, in the spirit, [and] not in the letter; whose praise [is] not of men, but of God." Romans 2:27-29.

No one is a Jew because he is circumcised outwardly, following the letter of the law. It must be in the heart to obey and believe, of inward actions of keeping the law out of love, not simply because it's the law.

"For we are the circumcision, which worship God in the spirit, and rejoice in Christ Jesus, and have no confidence in the flesh." Philippians 3:3

"Know therefore, that they which are of faith, the same are the children of Abraham." Galatians 3:7.

The A.D. 34 Shift

Knowing that only those who are Christ's are true members of Israel helps us to see that after A.D.34 at the stoning of Steven, we now change from a literal, geographical aspect of Israel to a spiritual, world-wide scope. Now that the geo-political Israel has rejected the Messiah, we have no choice but to see the prophecies of God fulfilling the new covenant promise in those who believe, wherever they might be in the world. The Israel of Christ's day rejected Him, as does the literal Israel of today.

So God has three choices, he can continue to use the Israel of today, choose another nation, or make His nation spiritual. The third choice should be clearly seen as what He has done.

We can't use the geographical nation of Israel of today, because they're a nation of people who mostly are still rejecting the Messiah. Clearly, the New Testament and history show us that God has regarded the church as His people, and His church only as they believe in the Deliverer. But beware, not all Israel are of Israel, not all the church is of the church.

Ellen White tells us who modern Israel is. We should easily see that she refers to the Seventh-day Adventist Church when she writes of the "Israel of today."

> "In order to be purified and to remain pure, <u>Seventh-day Adventists</u> must have the Holy Spirit in their hearts and in their homes. The Lord has given me light that when the <u>Israel of today</u> humble themselves before him, and cleanse the soul-temple from all defilement, he will hear their prayers in behalf of the sick, and will bless in the use of his remedies for disease. When in faith the human agent does all he can to combat disease, using the simple methods of treatment that God has provided, his efforts will be blessed of God." *Review and Herald*, March 3, 1910. Underlining supplied.

Why is This Important?

It's important for us to see that the physical, born-of-the-flesh Israel in the land of Palestine today, is not the Israel of God. This is for three reasons:

1. We must see that in Daniel 11:41, the meaning of "glorious land" is now the church, not the land of Israel. The blessings and curses of the Old Testament pertaining to Israel have been transferred to the Seventh-day Adventist Church. As not all Israel is of Israel and not all the church is of the church, not all Seventh-day Adventists are Seventh-day Adventists. There are many outside as well, and it's our duty to find them. Therefore, we should interpret Daniel 11, at the time of the end, to a spiritual Israel, not to the land of Israel in Palestine.

2. We need to understand this and be able to explain it to the rapture believers, which believe the Israel of today in Palestine is the recipient of the Old Testament promises. Those who believe the rapture doctrine must understand that the Israel of the Middle East today is not going to play a part in the fulfillment of the prophecies of the Old Testament for the last days. Instead, they will be deceived, waiting for the rapture and other events that won't happen, missing the real McCoy. In this case, the final atonement, the judgment.[2]

3. The role of the "numbered" 144,000 in Revelation will play out in the members of the Seventh-day Adventist Church, and does not represent the Jewish nation in Palestine today. The number 144,000 doesn't refer to all Christendom that accepts the message in the last days. No, there's another group represented by another name. The other faithful ones in the churches and other last minute converts who accept the third angel's message at the time of the end are represented by the "great multitude, which no man could number." Revelation 7:9.[3]

More on this later.

----

[1] Exodus 19:8, 24:3,7.

[2] Pastor Tim Roosenberg in his book *Islam & Christianity in Prophecy* presents the last great war between the king of the north and the king of the south as a war between the Papacy, supported by the United States, and Islam. As we will see later in this book, I don't agree with that scenario. If I am correct in by belief, then Pastor Rossenberg and his fellow believers will be waiting for a war that doesn't come. In the meantime, the final atonement, the judgment will come and pass them by. Please know for yourself what is truly coming in Daniel 11:40.

[3] For a better understanding of the numbered 144,000 and the un-numbered "great multitude", see the book, *Restoring the Holy of Holies, Revelation, a Seven-act Play* by this author. Available at your favorite bookstore or on the Internet.

Chapter 7
Rome and the Holy Covenant

In our study of Daniel 11, we're now dealing with Rome. Rome was the world power at the time of Christ, we should expect some mention at this point in Daniel 11 of the holy land or holy people. In a verse below, Daniel 11:28, we find the "holy covenant" mentioned. But first,

11:23 And after the league [made] with him he shall work deceitfully: for he shall come up, and shall become strong with a small people.

To some expositors, the word, "league" here is in question. Although similar in meaning, it's not the same word translated in Daniel 11:6 as "agreement." However, the translators of the KJV seem to be referring back to some previously mentioned "league" or "agreement." The definite article "the" is inserted, referring back to a previously mentioned "league." This would be the "league" or "agreement" of 161 B.C. that the Jews made with Rome.

In addition, in our discussion of verses previous to verse 23, we already reached the time of Christ and Tiberius Caesar in the first century A.D. The translation of the text here in verse 23 seems to be taking us back in time, back to a time already explained. In order to go back, Daniel has to refer us back to the "agreement" of B.C.161. He does this by mentioning the "agreement", but calls it by a similar word with a similar meaning, "the league." The text seems to be taking us back to that time and then continuing again to the Battle of Actium in B.C.31.

Rome worked "deceitfully," making treaties, agreements and leagues with nations and peoples only to get a foothold to gain control. Rome became the greatest of all world empires, starting from a city-state, a "small people."[1]

Tidings Out of the East

11:24 He shall enter peaceably even upon the fattest places of the province; and he shall do [that] which his fathers have not done, nor his fathers' fathers; he shall scatter among them the prey, and spoil, and riches: [yea], and he shall forecast his devices against the strong holds, even for a time.

Daniel 8:25 tells us this about Rome in a parallel verse.

"And through his [Rome's] policy also he shall cause craft to prosper in his hand; and he shall magnify [himself] in his heart, and by peace shall destroy many: he shall also stand up against the Prince of princes; but he shall be broken without hand."

The word "craft" in Strong's is also rendered, *deceiving, fraud, treachery, false* and *feigned*. Rome destroyed the surrounding countries in peace by pretending to be their friend and then taking them over from within. Rome was the first nation in history to gain control by such treachery. In this sense, "he shall do [that] which his fathers have not done." The previous world powers did it by war.

Rome was the world's leader, ruling with a rod of iron, as depicted by the iron legs of the image of Daniel 2. Her rule was "even for a time." This expression shows that time to be limited. Verses 27 and 29 use the term, for a "time appointed." God would set the limit; Rome would fall at God's chosen time.

11:25 And he shall stir up his power and his courage against the king of the south with a great army; and the king of the south shall be stirred up to battle with a very great and mighty army; but he shall not stand: for they shall forecast devices against him.

Here again we have a king from the south in battle. After the death of Julius Caesar, Rome was divided into two kingdoms, one headed by Augustus to the North of Palestine and the other, Mark Antony to the south, Egypt. As before, both directions were in reference to Palestine. Both had great armies, Augustus had the "very great and mighty army", but did "not stand", that is, come out the winner to take charge of Rome. Antony was defeated by actions from within, for "they shall forecast devices against him."

11:26 Yea, they that feed of the portion of his meat shall destroy him, and his army shall overflow: and many shall fall down slain.

Rome and the Holy Covenant - 7

In the battle of Actium in 31 B.C., Antony's forces deserted him, defecting to Augustus. Antony's forces had fed "of the portion of his [Antony's] meat."

11:27 And both these kings' hearts [shall be] to do mischief, and they shall speak lies at one table; but it shall not prosper: for yet the end [shall be] at the time appointed.

Here in history we are just before the Christian era, just before the coming of Jesus Christ. We are nearing the end of the 490 years, which were given to the Jews to get their house in order. This is the "time appointed," their probationary time of 490 years.

Against the Holy Covenant

Antony married Octovius' (Augustus Ceasar) sister, so they were brothers-in-law. Surely, they sat at the same table many times, speaking of their friendship, while both had "mischief" in mind. Marriage to Octavius' sister did not "prosper" Antony.

11:28 Then shall he return into his land with great riches; and his heart [shall be] against the holy covenant; and he shall do [exploits], and return to his own land.

The booty taken back to Rome was great. This act of being "against the holy covenant" could not be referring to Augustus taking action against the Jews. By this time, the Jews had already apostatized to a great degree. They were not keepers of the covenant and rejected their Messiah only 62 years after the decisive battle at Actium. They failed to meet the stipulations during the 490 years of probation.

On the other hand, think of it as Augustus returning to Rome after the battle. For many years, even going into the Christian era, Rome had no major battles to fight. Instead, she turned against the Christians, those who had picked up the banner of the "holy covenant" and were now carrying it into the Christian age. Rome turned against the Christians of whom alone it can be said were in compliance with the "Holy Covenant." This covenant was the promise God had made to Abraham. Later God spoke of the New Covenant.

The New Covenant

"Behold, the days come, saith the LORD, that I will make a new covenant with the house of Israel, and with the house of Judah. . . this [shall be] the covenant that I will make with the house of Israel; After those days, saith the LORD, I will put my law

Tidings Out of the East

in their inward parts, and write it in their hearts; and will be their God, and they shall be my people." Jeremiah 31"31-33.

Ellen White tells us this new covenant promise will be fulfilled in the investigative judgment. She says, "Thus will be realized the complete fulfillment of the new-covenant promise." She then quotes Jeremiah 31:34:50:20. This statement can be found in *The Great Controversy*, in the chapter entitled, "The Investigative Judgment," pages 484, 485.

The Jews had been blessed with the obligation to live and preach the "holy covenant", but failed to do so. At the stoning of Steven, in A.D.34 at the end of the 490 years, the gospel was passed on to the gentiles. Now, those that are His church are the keepers of the truth, the truth that is to be shared with the world.

Rome and its Caesars were now free from any outside power that might threaten them. They were free to do "exploits," although the word *exploits* is not in the text. They were "free to do" is more correct. He "returned to his own land," because there were no more wars to wage or armies to defeat. Augustus returned "to his own land" in peace.

Next, Rome changes her clothes.

---

[1] With this chapter, we're studying Daniel 11:23-28. The next chapter deals with Daniel 11:29-39. We must take note again that these verses are not as clearly understood, as we might want them to be, thereby not rendering as clear or unanimous opinion on what they are trying to teach us. As I count them, according to the books I've read, there are four different opinions. I wish there were just one, simple, clear explanation, but not so. I'm not satisfied entirely even with the view on these verses that I've put forth in this book. However, what really is important is what we understand when we deal with our two verses of focus, Daniel 11:40 and 11:44 and the verses in between. Who are the kings of the north and south? What is this battle? What are the tidings out of the east, and who is represented by the "Glorious Land"?

Chapter 8
Rome Changes Garbs

At this point in our study, we have passed the time of Christ and entered the Christian era. The children of Abraham refused to accept their Messiah, instead, they delivered Him up to the Romans. The 490-prophecy came to its end in A.D. 34, without the conditions being satisfied. Therefore, it was back to jail. They had to suffer the "curses" of Deuteronomy 28. The 2300-day "vision" was not sealed, so it continues to the fall of 1844.

However, we need a people to fulfill God's promise in the new covenant, His promise to Abraham. At Stephen's stoning at the end of the 490 years, the message started to go to the Gentiles. The Christian church, not the nation of Israel, was now the expectant recipient of the promise. Though the Jews were unfaithful, God was going to keep His Old Testament promises to Israel, by replacing Jews with Christians, grafting them into the olive tree.[1]

Therefore, in the following verses of Daniel 11, we need to read the "church" in the place of "Israel".

11:29 At the time appointed he shall return, and come toward the south; but it shall not be as the former, or as the latter.

What is the "time appointed?" It's the same time as in two verses back, the end of the 490 years of probationary time. However, "it shall not be as the former." When the king of the north comes again to the holy land, something has changed.

Many commentators want to interpret this as Constantine moving his capital to Constantinople in A.D. 330. But this is to the north and east, not to the south. The south should be Egypt, but history provides us with no event that could fulfill this prophecy. However, the verse gives us a clue. Something is different, "it shall not be as the former," not as before. What has changed?

Tidings Out of the East

At this time, beyond the "time appointed," God no longer has a nation in Palestine. Having entered the Christian dispensation, the meaning of Palestine has changed from geographical to spiritual. Israel is now the church consisting of the believers throughout the world. The name of Israel given to God's people now has a worldwide, universal meaning. The real Jews are those who believe in Jesus.[2]

In the same vein, the meaning of Egypt must change and be spiritual, not a geographic location. This is "not as it was before." Also, since expositors have not found any battle for this time between a king of the north and a king of the south, we find one more reason this kingdom must be a spiritual one.

In verse 29, the king of the north is passing through spiritual Israel to invade spiritual Egypt. We find a mention of spiritual Egypt in Revelation.[3]

> "The great city" in whose streets the witnesses are slain, and where their dead bodies lie, is "spiritually" Egypt. Of all nations presented in Bible history, Egypt most boldly denied the existence of the living God and resisted His commands. No monarch ever ventured upon more open and highhanded rebellion against the authority of Heaven than did the king of Egypt. When the message was brought him by Moses, in the name of the Lord, Pharaoh proudly answered: "Who is Jehovah, that I should hearken unto His voice to let Israel go? I know not Jehovah, and moreover I will not let Israel go." Exodus 5:2, A.R.V. *This is atheism*, and the nation represented by Egypt would give voice to a similar denial of the claims of the living God and would manifest a like spirit of unbelief and defiance. "The great city" is also compared, "spiritually," to Sodom. The corruption of Sodom in breaking the law of God was especially manifested in licentiousness. And this sin was also to be a pre-eminent characteristic of the nation that should fulfill the specifications of this scripture. *The Great Controversy*, 269. Emphasis supplied.

Here in *Great Controversy,* Ellen White is referring to the French Revolution. France spiritually attacked the Roman Catholic Church in the French Revolution of the late eighteenth century, taking the pope captive in 1798. The king of the north must also be changed. It was Papal Rome, and as we see by the little horn that came up in Daniel 7 and 8, it didn't take over by overthrowing another kingdom but came up out of Romanism, Pagan Rome. We know this as the Papacy, which came up from within the Roman system and carried on long after Pagan Rome dissolved into Papal Rome. Therefore, the Papacy became the king of the north. This is all confirmed in Daniel 7 and 8.

Pagan Rome is Papal Rome

Even though we speak of Pagan and Papal Rome, we need to see that for the most part they are really the same. Papal Rome kept its

Rome Changes Garbs - 8

religion, only changing the names of the Pagan gods, renaming them with the names of the apostles and prophets. In other words, Papal Rome is Paganism with Christian names.

In the Old Testament, the kingdom of the north was Babylon. Although to the east, to invade Palestine, and to avoid the desert to the east, Babylon had to come down "from the north."

> "For thus saith the Lord GOD; Behold, I will bring upon Tyrus Nebuchadrezzar king of Babylon, a king of kings, <u>from the north</u>, with horses, and with chariots, and with horsemen, and companies, and much people." Ezekiel 26:7. Underlining supplied.

Rome absorbed the lands and gods north of Palestine, creating within it a hodgepodge of beliefs, mainly from Babylon. In Revelation, the Papacy is the woman on the beast with the inscription on her forehead, "Mystery, Babylon the Great, The Mother of Harlots and Abominations of the Earth." Revelation 17:5. Therefore, we have spiritual Babylon, first, Pagan Rome, later, Pagan Rome going into a metamorphosis, adopting Christianity as its religion, becoming Papal Rome.

In place of literal Israel, we have spiritual Israel (Church) and instead of geographic Egypt, we have spiritual Egypt, Explained earlier in this chapter as Atheism. Since Pagan Rome didn't fully change into Papal Rome until around 538, the first few hundred years of this prophecy refers to Pagan Rome.

So, if the king of the north is the Papacy, the king of the south is atheism, and Israel is not in Palestine but the true people of God, His Church, then in verse 29, how does the king of the north invade the king of the south, spiritual Egypt?

Before the Papacy could gain full control of the world, it had to destroy the atheistic tribes, Barbarians, Vandals and others. When we look to Daniel 7, we see the ten horns coming out to the Roman Empire. We know that the last three had to be "plucked up" before Papal Rome could have it all. The last one being in A.D. 538.[4]

11:30 For the ships of Chittim shall come against him: therefore he shall be grieved, and return, and have indignation against the holy covenant: so shall he do; he shall even return, and have intelligence with them that forsake the holy covenant.

Tidings Out of the East

If since the beginning of the Christian era we are dealing with spiritual applications for the kings of the north and south and for Israel, we might expect a spiritual application for the "ships of Chittim." *The Seventh-day Adventist Bible Commentary* states they came to be applied in general to foreign oppressors.[5] History and prophecy tell us that the tens tribes of the ten horns of Daniel 7 gave Rome a hard time for many years, eventually bringing an end to Pagan Rome, opening the way to the Papacy, a nation with Pagan beliefs, cloaked in Christian nomenclature.

When Constantine ruled, starting in A.D.311, the Roman Empire was in decline. Christianity was growing to where something had to be done. The first centuries of Christianity brought torture, murder and unspeakable horrendous crimes perpetrated against Christians, but to no avail. The blood of martyrs is as seed. The more Christians died, the more their numbers grew. Constantine needed a solution, and Satan presented him with one.

Constantine claimed a miraculous conversion to the True God and set Christianity up as the official state religion, reuniting church and state. By doing so, he tried to bring the two forms of worship together, Paganism and Christianity. In this way, it was "against the holy covenant."

Compromise with error never brings error to the truth but embeds corruptive errors into the truth. Christianity fast filled up with Paganism disguised as Christianity. The church, the Roman Catholic Church, became spiritual Babylon while the woman, God's true church, fled into the wilderness. [6]

11:31 And arms shall stand on his part, and they shall pollute the sanctuary of strength, and shall take away the daily [sacrifice], and they shall place the abomination that makes desolate.

The word translated *arms* from the Hebrew should be translated *arm*, meaning the lower arm denoting strength. In one place, the same word is translated *arm*, "And the LORD brought us forth out of Egypt with a mighty hand, and with an outstretched arm." Deuteronomy 26:8.

The Roman Church took on the arm of the then present military power to enforce its laws and force man's will. They polluted the sanctuary and took away the "daily"[7] by setting up a Pagan system of priests that was contrary to the idea of Christ as our High Priest in the sanctuary in heaven. This effectually "took away" the true teaching of the tabernacle and the true High Priest, replacing it with a false

Rome Changes Garbs - 8

system, separating man from his God, corrupting the truth. They replaced the truth to the point of claiming all forgiveness is through the church, the priests and even through Mary.

"Abomination that Makes Desolate"

The worship of Sunday was instigated as the day of worship, thereby setting up "the abomination that makes desolate."

> "And the Saviour warned His followers: "When ye therefore shall see the abomination of desolation, spoken of by Daniel the prophet, stand in the holy place,...then let them which be in Judea flee into the mountains." Matthew 24:15, 16; Luke 21:20, 21. When the idolatrous standards of the Romans should be set up in the holy ground, which extended some furlongs outside the city walls, then the followers of Christ were to find safety in flight. When the warning sign should be seen, those who would escape must make no delay." *The Great Controversy*, p. 26.

Ellen white ties this in with the Sunday law.

> "... As the siege of Jerusalem by the Roman armies was the signal for flight to the Judean Christians, so the assumption of power on the part of our nation [the United States] in the decree enforcing the papal sabbath will be a warning to us." *Testimonies for the Church, v. 5*, p. 464-5.

The abomination that makes desolate occurs three times,

1. The destruction of Jerusalem in A.D. 70. Matthew 24:15, 16; Luke 21:20, 21; *Great Controversy*, 26, 464-5.
2. The Sunday law of Constantine's time, along with the false system of worship. Daniel 11:28.
3. The national Sunday law at the end of time. *Great Controversy*, 464-5.

11:32 And such as do wickedly against the covenant shall he corrupt by flatteries: but the people that do know their God <u>shall be strong</u>, and do [exploits].

Some try to corrupt the people with sweet talk. When that fails, they use force. Nevertheless, God's true people who know God "shall be strong." Although the Church of Rome misrepresented Christianity, carrying it into deep apostasy, faithful heroes such as the Albigenses and the Waldenses stood strong for truth. They carried parts of the Bible to many far and near, sharing the truth with whomever would hear. In this way, they would "do exploits."

Tidings Out of the East

11:33 And they that understand among the people shall instruct many: yet they shall fall by the sword, and by flame, by captivity, and by spoil, [many] days.

For 1260 years, the Papacy ran free to do its will. If it couldn't sway the people with sweet words that tickle the ears, it tried to do so with flame and sword. The Inquisition is infamous.

11:34 Now when they shall fall, they shall be helped with a little help: but many shall cleave to them with flatteries.

In the darkness of Papal supremacy, the Reformation was born. The truth was revived, but the Papacy didn't die. It's alive and well today. It's growing with every passing day, as Protestants forget what it means to be Protestant. The Papists now flatter us with the idea they have changed, that persecution is past and will not raise its ugly head again. Speaking of Rome changing, Ellen White says,

> "And this is the religion which Protestants are beginning to look upon with so much favor, and which will eventually be united with Protestantism. This union will not, however, be effected by a change in Catholicism; for <u>Rome never changes</u>. She claims infallibility. It is Protestantism that will change." Review and Herald, June 1, 1886. Underlining supplied.

11:35 And [some] of them of understanding shall fall, to try them, and to purge, and to make [them] white, [even] to the time of the end: because [it is] yet for a time appointed.

Many of the great teachers, the reformers, were killed during the Reformation. They were tried and tested and were made white through the justifying and sanctifying grace of God. They taught that only through the gospel they could be forgiven and changed, not through or by the Roman church. However, the time of the end was not yet upon them. They needed to wait until the "time appointed." The previous "time appointed" was the end of the 490 years, the time when God had planned that Israel end its backsliding and "seal up the vision." Since they failed to do so, the "time appointed" now changes to the time of the end, 1798, and on to 1844.

11:36 And the king shall do according to his will; and he shall exalt himself, and magnify himself above every god, and shall speak marvelous things against the God of gods, and shall prosper till the indignation be accomplished: for that that is determined shall be done.

Rome Changes Garbs - 8

We find this paralleled in Daniel 7:25. The "indignation" in Daniel 11 corresponds to the 1260 years, "time and times and the dividing of time," of Daniel 8. The little horn is the king of the north. Here's what it says about the little horn,

> "And he shall speak [great] words against the most High, and shall wear out the saints of the most High, and think to change times and laws: and they shall be given into his hand until a time and times and the dividing of time." Daniel 7:25.

Few opposed the Papacy until the Reformation. The popes were kings over the church and its people. Paul wrote of the man of sin,

> "Let no man deceive you by any means: for [that day shall not come], except there come a falling away first, and that man of sin be revealed, the son of perdition; Who opposes and exalts himself above all that is called God, or that is worshipped; so that he as God sits in the temple of God, showing himself that he is God." 2 Thessalonians 2:3, 4.

The "indignation" is the anger of God toward the sins instigated and committed though the centuries by the man of sin. God permitted them, but set a time for their end. It's the "time of the end," 1798, and on to 1844 when "the judgment was set and the books were opened" Daniel 7:10. At this time the man of sin, the "little horn" will be destroyed, ". . . the judgment shall sit, and they shall take away his dominion, to consume and to destroy [it] unto the end." Daniel 7:26. It's the cleansing of the sanctuary, the final atonement.

11:37 Neither shall he regard the God of his fathers, nor the desire of women, nor regard any god: for he shall magnify himself above all.

He would not regard the God of his fathers, Jehovah, the "desire of women", which is the Desire of Ages. He "magnified" and worshipped himself alone, saying that he was God. To this day, the popes of Rome claim to be Christ in the flesh. They are called the Vicar of Christ. A name that was given the popes early in history is Vicarius Filii Dei,[8] meaning *in place of the son of God*.

11:38 But in his estate shall he honor the God of forces: and a god whom his fathers knew not shall he honor with gold, and silver, and with precious stones, and pleasant things.

The Papacy is more than a religious entity. Even though it has no army of its own, it's also a political regime that honors force, military force to do its biddings. In the time of Rome, it used the forces of

Tidings Out of the East

Rome. Later, when it controlled other secular forces, it used them. Although Satan uses force, God never forces the conscience. Revenge is God's prerogative, but He seldom uses it. He prefers to draw men to Him through His love. Jeremiah wrote, "The LORD hath appeared of old unto me, [saying], Yea, I have loved thee with an everlasting love: therefore with loving kindness have I drawn thee." Jeremiah 31:3.

A forced convert is a reluctant convert is no convert at all. The world has too many convinced, yet unconverted Christians. Controlling through force would be an easy thing for God, but force would not endear us to Him.

11:39 Thus shall he do in the most strong holds with a strange god, whom he shall acknowledge [and] increase with glory: and he shall cause them to rule over many, and shall divide the land for gain.

The Papacy spread its tentacles throughout the known world in the form of priests, bishops and archbishops. The best way to control is from the top down, using those below as spies to report to the higher ranks. Such a pyramid structure is a totalitarian tool in the hands of the popes. Orders come from the top down, while reports of obedience or disobedience come from the bottom up. Individual ideas and new thoughts are under the control of the upper echelons. Dissention is easy to control. To disagree with the leadership brings on separation from the main body.

This form of governing is a military form of regime. However, with true Christianity and Protestantism, God deals directly with the believer, teaching doctrine and leading the sinner into God's plan for them. It's God and the Scriptures. It doesn't come to each individual from or through the church, but directly from God. We have but one leader. "But be not ye called Rabbi: for one is your Master, [even] Christ; and <u>all ye are brethren</u>." Matthew 23:8. Underlining supplied.

"No man is a proper judge of another man's duty. Man is responsible to God; and as finite, erring men take into their hands the jurisdiction of their fellowmen, as if the Lord commissioned them to lift up and cast down, all heaven is filled with indignation. There are strange principles being established in regard to the control of the minds and works of men, by human judges, as though these finite men were gods." *Testimonies to Ministers*, p. 349

The Jews in Jesus day and the Roman Church through the dark ages took the wrong attitude toward the Scriptures. We must be careful not to do the same. Speaking of the church today, the prophet warns us,

Rome Changes Garbs - 8

"How shall we search the Scriptures in order to understand what they teach? . . . We are not to think, as did the Jews, that our own ideas and opinions are infallible; nor with the papists, that certain individuals are the sole guardians of truth and knowledge, that men have no right to search the Scriptures for themselves, but must accept the explanations given by the fathers of the church. . . .

"Some have feared that if in even a single point they acknowledge themselves in error, other minds would be led to doubt the whole theory of truth. Therefore they have felt that investigation should not be permitted, that it would tend to dissension and disunion. But if such is to be the result of investigation, the sooner it comes the better. If there are those whose faith in God's word will not stand the test of an investigation of the Scriptures, the sooner they are revealed the better; for then the way will be opened to show them their error. . . .

"Those who allow prejudice to bar the mind against the reception of truth cannot receive the divine enlightenment. Yet, when a view of Scripture is presented, many do not ask, Is it true--in harmony with God's word? but, By whom is it advocated? and unless it comes through the very channel that pleases them, they do not accept it. So thoroughly satisfied are they with their own ideas that they will not examine the Scripture evidence with a desire to learn, but refuse to be interested, merely because of their prejudices.

"The Lord often works where we least expect Him; He surprises us by revealing His power through instruments of His own choice, while He passes by the men to whom we have looked as those through whom light should come. God desires us to receive the truth upon its own merits--because it is truth . . .

"But beware of rejecting that which is truth. The great danger with our people has been that of depending upon men and making flesh their arm. Those who have not been in the habit of searching the Bible for themselves, or weighing evidence, have confidence in the leading men and accept the decisions they make; and thus many will reject the very messages God sends to His people, if these leading brethren do not accept them.

". . . Even if all our leading men should refuse light and truth, that door will still remain open. The Lord will raise up men who will give the people the message for this time." *Testimonies to Ministers*, 105-107.

How we determine the time of the end and what happens at that time is next.

----

[1] Roman 11:16-26
[2] See Galatians 3:29
[3] See Revelation 11:8
[4] See Daniel 7:8
[5] See SDABC on Numbers 24:24
[6] Revelation 12:6
[7] The two most popular views on the meaning of the "daily" are explained later in this book.
[8] Add up this name, Vicarius Filii Dei, in Roman numerals; it comes to 666. see the next page.

The Number of His Name
Revelation 13:18

The Number of His Name
V I C A R I U S
5 1 100   1 5 = 112
F I L I I
112   1 50 1 1 = 53
53
501   D E I
666   500 1 = 501

Chapter 9
The Time of the End

If we had read Daniel's prophecy in his time, we, too, would have been left in the dark. From what Daniel was shown in vision, there's little or nothing in Daniel 11 that would help us see what was to come, but from the reverse angle of history, from our time, we can open the history books and look back, finding historical events that apply to each part of the prophecy. Surely, God gave us this prophecy with the plan for our day. The angel told Daniel,

> "But thou, O Daniel, shut up the words, and seal the book, [even] to the time of the end: many shall run to and fro, and knowledge shall be increased." Daniel 12:4.

Today, the knowledge of science and technology has increased exponentially. However, this "increase in knowledge" has the primary meaning of understanding the prophecies of Daniel. Since Daniel's prophecies are known today, it follows that we are in the "time of the end," the time the prophecies were to be unsealed.

But why is it necessary to know so much history? Why do we have to go through so much effort to know? Think on this, only those who search, God's true people, will take the time to find out the truth. They will understand, "the wise shall understand."

In a few verses farther down in Daniel 12, the angel said to Daniel,

> "Many shall be purified, and made white, and tried; but the wicked shall do wickedly: and none of the wicked shall understand; but <u>the wise shall understand</u>." Daniel 12:10.

God's eternal purpose has been to restore His people to the position they held before sin entered this world. What was lost in Eden will be reclaimed and restored at the end of time. God's true

Tidings Out of the East

people "*shall understand.*" The book of Daniel is about restoration. God will restore His people. He will restore His sanctuary, He will restore His kingdom and finally, He will restore the King.

Our Secondary Text of Focus - Daniel 11:40

Here is our secondary text of focus that we have been leading up to. It's about the king of the north and the king of the south at the "time of the end."

11:40 And at the time of the end shall the king of the south push at him: and the king of the north shall come against him like a whirlwind, with chariots, and with horsemen, and with many ships; and he shall enter into the countries, and shall overflow and pass over.

The "time of the end" is mentioned earlier in Daniel 12:4. It's the time the prophecies of Daniel would be unsealed. This happened at the end of the 1260 years of Papal supremacy in 1798. In the early 1800's, William Miller started his study of Daniel, leading up to the prediction of the 2300 days concluding in 1844.

As we view this scene of Daniel 11:40, we need to see ourselves in the land of Palestine, for where else could we be? The king to the south would be Egypt, but Egypt did nothing worth noting at this time at the end of the 1260 years in 1798 or even near 1844.

Nevertheless, starting at the French Revolution, there was something brewing that for many years would affect the socio-economic systems of the world, Communism. Karl Marx was born in 1818 and wrote his *Communist Manifesto* in 1848. Its foundation was atheism which was given a boost by Charles Darwin in his theories on evolution. Darwin's *Origin of the Species* was published in 1859. On October 9, 2012 the following statement was on the Internet.

> "Washington (CNN) - the fastest growing "religions" group in America is made up of people with no religion at all, according to a Pew survey showing that one in five Americans is not affiliated with any religion."

Atheism is Egypt, but not the country in the Middle East today; it's spiritual Egypt. Ellen White equates Egypt with Atheism in her description of the French Revolution. Please read again the quote on page 42 of this book. This *Great Controversy*, page 269 statement can be found in the chapter on the French Revolution occurring from 1789-1799. It was just at the end of the 1260 years that ended in 1798. Atheism grew and extended its arms to Russia, China and even to the

United States. But what connection does France have with Atheism? Ellen White, quoting *Blackwood's Magazine* says this,

> "France stands apart in the world's history as the single state which, by the decree of her Legislative Assembly, pronounced that there was no God, and of which the entire population of the capital, and a vast majority elsewhere, women as well as men, danced and sang with joy in accepting the announcement."--Blackwood's Magazine, November, 1870." *Great Controversy*, p. 269.

So, this is what we have, the king of the south, Atheism, pushes at the king of the north, Papacy, but the Papacy overcomes the attack. While believing this more than forty years ago, I made the prediction that Communism would fall in Russia through the power of the Catholic Church, mostly from within Communism itself. This happened in 1989 when the USSR tried to put down protests in Poland. The Papacy pushed back, not only clearing Poland of Communism, Atheism, but also brought an end to the Soviet Union itself.

The fight is not over, but in the end, the two powers, Catholicism and Atheism, fighting for supremacy will be against the truth, the Holy People. The kings of the north and south will fight each other, with spiritual Israel in the middle. The Papacy will win against Atheism. Atheism is pushing at the king of the north even now, as Catholicism and Christianity in general are losing ground to a world of god-less people. But it won't be long until the Papacy turns its entire strength against God's people.

When the condition of the economy worsens seriously and natural disasters increase exceedingly, then Protestant America will look for a means to stop the bleeding. This will result in the Sunday law. As it is said, there are no atheists in foxholes; there will be no atheists on the earth, for everyone will be involved. This will be the great conflict, symbolized by the mark of the beast and the seal of God.

Although the Papacy led by the popes received a deadly wound in 1798 when atheist France "pushed at him" by taking the pope captive, it will eventually come to pass that, ". . . his deadly wound was [is] healed: and all the world wondered after the beast." Revelation 13:3.

Understanding the Conflict

We must see this conflict between the king of the north and the king of the south as between the Roman church and Atheism, not between the world of Islam or Turkey or China. If the two kings are truly represent the Papacy and Atheism as explained in this book, then those of who believe otherwise will be waiting for a non-event, passed

Tidings Out of the East

by without a clue. This prophecy of Daniel must be studied and understood clearly. We need to be well informed and ready.

Parallels in Daniel 8 and 11,12

Daniel 8		Daniel 11-12	
Persia, ram	v.3,20	Persia, king	v/2
Greece, he-goat	v.5,21	Greece, king	v.3; cf. v.2
Four Winds, Great horn broken		Four Winds, Mighty king	vs.3
toward four winds	v.8	Rules with great dominion	v.3
		Kingdome broken	v.4
		Toward the 4 winds of heaven	v.4
Pagan Rome,	v.9	Pagan Rome,	
Trampled on the host	v.10	Robbers of thy people	v.14
Christian Rome,		Christian Rome	
The little horn	v.9	King of the north	v.29
"Daily" taken away.		"Daily" taken away	v.31
Sanctuary cast down.	v.11	Sanctuary profaned	v.31
Practices and prospers	v.12	Prospers	v.36
Cast the truth to the ground.	v.12	Works deceitfully	v.23
End of the time appointed	v.19	End at time appointed	v.27,35
Becomes mighty	v.24	Strong with small people	v.23
Destroys wonderfully	v.24	Great fury to destroy	v.44
Destroys holy people	v.25	Wise fall by the sword	v.33
Causes craft to prosper	v.25	Corrupts by flatteries	v.32
Magnifies himself	v.25	Magnifies himself, speaks against God	v.4
		Tidings from the east	v.44
Broken without hand	v.25	Michael stands up	12:2

Chapter 10
The Glorious Land

This chapter is one that I would rather not write, but Isaiah admonishes me to do so. He wrote, "Cry aloud, spare not, lift up thy voice like a trumpet, and show my people their transgression, and the house of Jacob their sins." Isaiah 58:1. Ellen White corroborates,

"Who are standing in the counsel of God at this time? Is it those who virtually excuse wrongs among the professed people of God and who murmur in their hearts, if not openly, against those who would reprove sin? Is it those who take their stand against them and sympathize with those who commit wrong? No, indeed! Unless they repent, and leave the work of Satan in oppressing those who have the burden of the work and in holding up the hands of sinners in Zion, they will never receive the mark of God's sealing approval. They will fall in the general destruction of the wicked, represented by the work of the five men bearing slaughter weapons. Mark this point with care: Those who receive the pure mark of truth, wrought in them by the power of the Holy Ghost, represented by a mark by the man in linen, are those "that sigh and that cry for all the abominations that be done" in the church. Their love for purity and the honor and glory of God is such, and they have so clear a view of the exceeding sinfulness of sin, that they are represented as being in agony, even sighing and crying. Read the ninth chapter of Ezekiel. *Testimonies*, vol.3, 267. Emphasis supplied.

To understand the next verse, Daniel 11:41, we have to see that the enemy will enter into the "glorious land." We need to stand up as Daniel's three friends did in ancient Babylon, and as Daniel did with the king's law that got him thrown into the den of lions. We, too, might be headed for the furnace or the lion's den, but we must be willing to go there, if need be.

11:41 He shall enter also into the glorious land, and many [countries] shall be overthrown: but these shall escape out of his hand, [even] Edom, and Moab, and the chief of the children of Ammon.

Tidings Out of the East

The "glorious land" is the land of Palestine, but no longer is it a geographical location. The "glorious land" today is the true church, the true people of God, the advent movement. It's the Seventh-day Adventist Church.

In the above verse, the word "countries" is supplied by the translators. It's not in the Hebrew text. So, are we to believe that the Papacy, the king of the north, is going to overthrow many within the Seventh-day Adventist Church?

It's rather absurd to think that all members within the church are on the right track to heaven, and that none will lose their way. Adventists pastors everywhere will tell you that not all SDA's will be saved. Paul put it this way, "Not all of Israel are of Israel." Let me extend it to our day and say, not all Seventh-day Adventists are Seventh-day Adventists.

As Daniel wrote, "He [king of the north] shall enter also into the glorious land, [SDA Church] and many . . . shall be overthrown." Satan will infiltrate the remnant church to deceive and cause many to perish. Not all Israel is of Israel, not all Seventh-day Adventists are Seventh-day Adventists. Some will be destroyed in the last days. Read Ezekiel 9.

Ezekiel 9

In the quotation on the previous page, Ellen White tells us to "Read the ninth chapter of Ezekiel." *Testimonies*, vol.3, 267. Here is Ezekiel 9,

"He cried also in mine ears with a loud voice, saying, Cause them that have charge over the city to draw near, even every man [with] his destroying weapon in his hand. And, behold, six men came from the way of the higher gate, which lies <u>toward the north</u>, and every man a slaughter weapon in his hand; and one man among them [was] clothed with linen, with a writer's inkhorn by his side: and they went in, and stood beside the brazen altar. . . And he called to the man clothed with linen, which [had] the writer's inkhorn by his side; And the LORD said unto him, Go through the midst of the city, through the midst of Jerusalem, and <u>set a mark upon the foreheads of the men that sigh and that cry for all the abominations that be done in the midst thereof</u>. And to the others he said in mine hearing, Go ye after him through the city, and smite: let not your eye spare, neither have ye pity: Slay utterly old [and] young, both maids, and little children, and women: but come not near any man upon whom [is] the mark; and <u>begin at my sanctuary</u>. Then they began at the ancient men which [were] before the house. And he said unto them, Defile the house, and fill the courts with the slain: go ye forth. And they went forth, and slew in the city. And it came to pass, while they were slaying them, and I was left, that I fell upon my face, and cried, and said, Ah Lord GOD! will you destroy all the residue of Israel in thy pouring out of your fury upon Jerusalem? Then said he unto me, The iniquity of the house of Israel

The Glorious Land - 10

and Judah [is] exceeding great, and the land is full of blood, and the city full of perverseness: for they say, The LORD hath forsaken the earth, and the LORD sees not. And as for me also, mine eye shall not spare, neither will I have pity, [but] I will recompense their way upon their head. And, behold, the man clothed with linen, which [had] the inkhorn by his side, reported the matter, saying, I have done as thou hast commanded me." Ezekiel 9:1-11. Underlining supplied.

We need to get four important points from Ezekiel 9,

1. The men come from the north to seal or slaughter. This corresponds to Daniel where he writes, "But tidings out of the east and out of the north shall trouble him. . ." Daniel 11:44. Later in this chapter, we'll learn that these tidings are the third angel's message concerning the seal of God. Along with the message of good tidings, men come with slaughter weapons. The message of tidings are the seal or mark, pass or fail. Which side we are on will be determined.

2. Those that receive the seal are they that ". . . sigh and that cry for all the abominations that be done in the midst thereof." Ellen White changes the wording just slightly, but it clarifies who she believes is being targeted. She writes,

"Those who receive the pure mark of truth, wrought in them by the power of the Holy Ghost, represented by a mark by the man in linen, are those "that sigh and that cry for all the abominations that be done" in the church. . . .Read the ninth chapter of Ezekiel. *Testimonies*, vol.3, 267. Emphasis supplied.

Yes, it's the church, not the Roman Catholic Church, but the Seventh-day Adventist Church. After all, she wrote the *Testimonies* for the SDA Church, and are called *Testimonies for the Church*.

3. Ezekiel 9 tells us the judgment begins, "at my sanctuary." Peter wrote, "For the time [is come] that judgment must begin <u>at the house of God</u>: and if [it] first [begin] at us, what shall the end [be] of them that obey not the gospel of God?" 1 Peter 4:17. The SDA Church will first be judged, numbered and sealed to be among the 144,000. This number is mentioned first in Revelation 7,

"And I saw another angel ascending from the east, having the seal of the living God: and he cried with a loud voice to the four angels, to whom it was given to hurt the earth and the sea, Saying, Hurt not the earth, neither the sea, nor the trees, till we have sealed the servants of our God in their foreheads. And I heard the number of them which were sealed: [and there were] sealed an hundred [and] forty [and] four thousand of all the tribes of the children of Israel." Revelation 7:2-4.

The 144,000 will later be joined by the "great multitude."

"After this I beheld, and, lo, a great multitude, which no man could number, of all nations, and kindreds, and people, and tongues, stood before the throne, and before the Lamb, clothed with white robes, and palms in their hands;" Revelation 7:9.

The 144,000 come from Modern Israel, the SDA Church. Later, the great multitude are from ". . . all nations, and kindreds and people and tongues." Revelation 7:9.

4. Finally, the angel with the writer's inkhorn, the sealing angel, comes to report, "I have done as thou hast commanded." This is the judgment. Speaking again from Ezekiel 9, the prophet tells us,

"I saw angels hurrying to and fro in heaven. An angel with a writer's inkhorn by his side returned from the earth and reported to Jesus that his work was done, and the saints were numbered and sealed. Then I saw Jesus, who had been ministering before the ark containing the ten commandments, throw down the censer. He raised His hands, and with a loud voice said, "It is done." And all the angelic host laid off their crowns as Jesus made the solemn declaration, "He that is unjust, let him be unjust still: and he which is filthy, let him be filthy still: and he that is righteous, let him be righteous still: and he that is holy, let him be holy still." Early Writings, 279.

This is the final judgment. It's over the seal of God and the mark of the beast. Those that are sealed among God's Seventh-day Adventist people will be spared, but not those "in the church" that are dealt with by the men with slaughter weapons. It's not clear how literal this slaughtering is. If we take it for what it implies, we would seriously have to think it means death. On the other hand, maybe it's just separation for the main body. In any case, some "in the church" are on the wrongs side of the issue at hand.

1888

Is this possible? Has some power *cut the cable* that anchored them to the Rock? Have we not heard of the 1888 conference, where the message was rejected? Have we or have we not been living up to the calling that is ours?

Just months before the 1888 conference was held, the following statement from Ellen White came out.

"Spiritual death has come upon the people that should be manifesting life and zeal, purity and consecration, by the most earnest devotion to the cause of truth. The facts concerning the real condition of the professed people of God, speak more loudly than their profession, and make it evident that <u>some power has cut the cable</u> that anchored them to the Eternal Rock, and that they are drifting away to sea, without chart or compass." Review and Herald, July 24, 1888. Underling supplied.

The Precious Message of 1888.

"The Lord in His great mercy sent a most precious message to His people through Elders Waggoner and Jones. This message was to bring more prominently before the world the uplifted Saviour, the sacrifice for the sins of the whole world. It presented justification through faith in the Surety; it invited the people to receive the righteousness of Christ, which is made manifest in obedience to all the commandments of God. Many had lost sight of Jesus. . . This is the message that God commanded to be given to the world. It is the third angel's message, which is to be proclaimed with a loud voice, and attended with the outpouring of His Spirit in a large measure." *Testimonies to Ministers*, 91.

"In Minneapolis God gave precious gems of truth to His people in new settings, This light from heaven by some was rejected with all the stubbornness the Jews manifested in rejecting Christ, and there was much talk about standing by the old landmarks. But there was evidence they knew not what the old landmarks were. . . .

"The men in responsible positions have disappointed Jesus. They have refused precious blessings, and refused to be channels of light, as He wanted them to be. The knowledge they should receive of God that they might be a light and blessing to others, they refuse to accept, and thus become channels of darkness. The spirit of God is grieved. . . . "11 Manuscript Release, 243.

"The perils of the last days are upon us. Satan takes the control of every mind that is not decidedly under the control of the Spirit of God. Some have been cultivating hatred against the men whom God has commissioned to bear a special message to the world. They began this satanic work at Minneapolis. Afterward, when they saw and felt the demonstration of the Holy Spirit testifying that the message was of God, they hated it the more, because it was a testimony against them. They would not humble their hearts to repent, to give God the glory, and vindicate the right. They went on in their own spirit, filled with envy, jealousy, and evil surmisings, as did the Jews. They opened their hearts to the enemy of God and man. Yet these men have been holding positions of trust, and have been molding the work after their own similitude, as far as they possibly could. . . . " *Testimonies to Ministers*, 79.

"The prejudices and opinions that prevailed at Minneapolis are not dead by any means; the seeds sown there in some hearts are ready to spring into life and bear a like harvest. The tops have been cut down, but the roots have never been eradicated, and they still bear their unholy fruit to poison the judgment, pervert the perceptions, and blind the understanding of those with whom you connect, in regard to the message and the messengers. " *Testimonies to Ministers*, 467.

The message of 1888 should have gone quickly throughout the world. In spite the many books written since 1888 saying the message was finally accepted, it was not. If it had been, we wouldn't be here today.[1]

Tidings Out of the East

Not only has it not been accepted, it's still not understood. When the message of 1888 is finally understood and accepted, the work will go fast. God will finish the work.

"For he [God] will finish the work, and cut [it] short in righteousness: because a short work will the Lord make upon the earth." Romans 9:28.

"When divine power is combined with human effort, the work will spread like fire in the stubble. God will employ agencies whose origin man will be unable to discern. Angels will do a work which men might have had the blessing of accomplishing had they not neglected to answer the claims of God." *Selected Messages*, Book 1, 118 (1885).

The Omega of Apostasy

In the early years of the twentieth century, John Harvey Kellogg brought a heresy into the Seventh-day Adventist Church. It was named the *alpha* of apostasy. It was Pantheism, the belief that God is in everything. To have God in us, Pantheism teaches we merely have to breath the God-filled air or drink the God-filled water. Ellen White recognized this apostasy for what it was and predicted an *omega* heresy would come later. Omega is the last letter of the Greek alphabet, so we should expect the omega to be the last heresy before the second coming.

"Be not deceived; many will depart from the faith, giving heed to seducing spirits and doctrines of devils. We have now before us the alpha of this danger. The omega will be of a most startling nature." 1 *Selected Messages*, 197.

Not much was said or written by Ellen White as to what the omega might be, except for the quotation that follows. It's mentioned in the next paragraph after the quotation quoted above about the omega.

"We need to study the words that Christ uttered in the prayer that He offered just before His trial and crucifixion. "These words spake Jesus, and lifted up his eyes to heaven, and said, Father, the hour is come; glorify thy Son, that thy Son also may glorify thee: as thou hast given him power over all flesh, that he should give eternal life to as many as thou hast given him. And this is life eternal, that they might know thee the only true God, and Jesus Christ, whom thou hast sent. I have glorified thee on the earth: I have finished the work which thou gave me to do. And now, O Father, glorify thou me with thine own self with the glory which I had with thee before the world was. I have manifested thy name unto the men which thou gave me out of the world: thine they were, and thou gave them me; and they have kept thy word" (John 17:1-6)." 1 Selected Messages, 197, 198..

What could John 17 have to do with the omega apostasy? To answer, let's ask how Jesus glorified His Father. He did so by representing God and His goodness to the watching universe. Jesus did it by living a perfect life in perfect harmony with His Father's will and His laws.

How can God's people do the same? They will have the opportunity and special privilege of being numbered and sealed among the 144,000, being tempted through the time of trouble as Jesus was in the wilderness, and then finally overcoming all temptations to show the on-looking universe that God is love, the justifier and sanctifier of all who will put their trust in Him. Jesus is our example. He, as a man, showed that men and women can live a perfect life, if God is with them. If we live as He lived and receive the Holy Spirit to the full as He did, what Jesus did, we can also do.

Ellen White's Comments on John 17

"With strong, hopeful words the Saviour ended His instruction. Then He poured out the burden of His soul in prayer for His disciples. Lifting His eyes to heaven, He said, 'Father, the hour is come; glorify Thy Son, that Thy Son also may glorify Thee: as Thou hast given Him power over all flesh, that He should give eternal life to as many as Thou hast given Him. And this is life eternal, that they might know Thee the only true God, and Jesus Christ, whom Thou hast sent.'

"Christ had finished the work that was given Him to do. He had glorified God on the earth. He had manifested the Father's name. He had gathered out those who were to continue His work among men. And He said, 'I am glorified in them. And now I am no more in the world, but these are in the world, and I come to Thee. Holy Father, keep through Thine own name those whom Thou hast given Me, that they may be one, as We are. Neither pray I for these alone, but for them also which shall believe on Me through their word; that they all may be one; . . . I in them, and Thou in Me, that they may be made perfect in one; and that the world may know that Thou hast sent Me, and hast loved them, as Thou hast loved Me.'

"Thus in the language of one who has divine authority, Christ gives His elect church into the Father's arms. As a consecrated high priest He intercedes for His people. As a faithful shepherd He gathers His flock under the shadow of the Almighty, in the strong and sure refuge. For Him there waits the last battle with Satan, and He goes forth to meet it." *Desire of Ages*, 680.

At this point, the sealed 144,000 are one with God, restored to perfection of character. Jesus was successful, being one with God. He then asked that His followers be afforded the opportunity to do the same. He asked to be one with them. Finally, Ellen White speaks of Jesus in the sanctuary where the last battle will take place. The omega, the last heresy, concerns the sanctuary. The omega is working to keep this union from happening.[2] Nevertheless, God's plan is that we, like Adam before his sin, will one day soon walk with Him in the garden in the cool of the day.

Tidings Out of the East

Satan is using the omega of apostasy to blind the minds of God's people from the final atonement, an atonement that will make God's people one with Him.

> "Satan is now using every device in this sealing time to keep the minds of God's people from the present truth and to cause them to waver. I saw a covering that God was drawing over His people to protect them in the time of trouble; and every soul that was decided on the truth and was pure in heart was to be covered with the covering of the Almighty." *Early Writings*, 43.

The Omega will be of a "most starling nature." What could be more startling than the turning away from the very message the Lord has given to the Seventh-day Adventist Church to promulgate? What message is that? It's the message of the final atonement, the message that God is going to perfect His people so they can go through the time of trouble without a mediator. It's the message of Daniel 8:14, the cleansing of the sanctuary.

Yes, the omega will come. In fact, Omega has come. It's infecting the Seventh-day Adventist Church. "Many shall be overthrown." Because of the omega, many will be shaken out.

Laodicea - The Shaking of Adventism

After all, we are Laodicea. The last of the seven churches in Revelation parallels the last six verses in Daniel 11. Laodicea means, "Judging the people." Daniel means, "God is Judge." The "tidings out of the east" tell of the judgment, the seal of the living God. It's God's final message to the church and the world. Those who are shaken out are so because they refuse to listen to the message of the True Witness to the Laodiceans. Here is that message.

> "I asked the meaning of the shaking I had seen and was shown that it would be caused by the straight testimony called forth by the counsel of the True Witness to the Laodiceans. This will have its effect upon the heart of the receiver, and will lead him to exalt the standard and pour forth the straight truth. Some will not bear this straight testimony. <u>They will rise up against it, and this is what will cause a shaking among God's people.</u>
> "I saw that the testimony of the True Witness has not been half heeded. The solemn testimony upon which the destiny of the church hangs has been lightly esteemed, if not entirely disregarded. This testimony must work deep repentance; all who truly receive it will obey it and be purified." Early Writings, 270. Underlining supplied.

What will happen with those who fail to heed the message? "They will rise up against it, and this is what will cause a shaking among

God's people." How much of this is caused by the leaders? Are we to trust the leadership? The leaders rebelled just before the Israelites went into the Promised Land. The leaders were responsible for the captivity in Babylon. The leaders caused the rejection of the Messiah. The leaders fought Luther and others during the Reformation, and it was the leaders who failed us in 1888, so can we trust the leaders today? Only if they are heeding the testimony of the True Witness, which has been only "half heeded." We must not follow their leading unless they are following God's leading. We are not to follow them simply because they are leading. We need to check out everything for ourselves.

The Very Last Deception of Satan

Ellen White tells us of the "very last deception of Satan." After reading the quotations below, can anyone believe the testimonies God has given us through Sister White are not necessary for us in these last days?

"Satan is . . . constantly pressing in the spurious--to lead away from the truth. *The very last deception of Satan will be to make of none effect the testimony of the Spirit of God.* "Where there is no vision, the people perish" (Proverbs 29:18). Satan will work ingeniously, in different ways and through different agencies, to unsettle the confidence of God's remnant people in the true testimony."-- Letter 12, 1890. 1 *Selected Messages*, 48.

"There will be a hatred kindled against the testimonies which is satanic. The workings of Satan will be to unsettle the faith of the churches in them, for this reason: Satan cannot have so clear a track to bring in his deceptions and bind up souls in his delusions if the warnings and reproofs and counsels of the Spirit of God are heeded."-- Letter 40, 1890. 1 *Selected Messages*, 48.

Furthermore, to take away any doubt concerning the importance of the spirit of prophecy, God's gift to us through the prophet Ellen White, read on,

"Men may get up scheme after scheme and the enemy will seek to seduce souls from the truth, but all who believe that the Lord has spoken through Sister White and has given her a message will be safe from the many delusions that will come in these last days."--*Selected Messages*, Book 3, 83, 84 (1906). *Last Day Events*, 44.

"It is Satan's plan to weaken the faith of God's people in the Testimonies. Next follows skepticism in regard to the vital points of our faith, the pillars of our position, then doubt as to the Holy Scriptures, and then the downward march to perdition. When the Testimonies, which were once believed, are doubted and given up, Satan knows the deceived ones will not stop at this; and he redoubles his efforts till he

Tidings Out of the East

launches them into open rebellion, which becomes incurable and ends in destruction." *Testimonies for the Church*, v. 4, 211.

God inspired the Testimonies and gave them to us through Ellen White. Some doubters can quote even Sister White where it might appear she down plays their importance, but all those statements are clearly trumped by these just quoted. Satan wants to destroy the messages given to God's last-day prophet, but because he cannot, he tries to get us to make of them "none effect," that is to say, ignore them and fail to use them. Interestingly enough, some members use them when they want to support their point, but immediately down play them when their opposition tries to use them to prove their point. We must believe and use them for what they were intended. We must believe whom God has sent.

"And they rose early in the morning, and went forth into the wilderness of Tekoa: and as they went forth, Jehoshaphat stood and said, Hear me, O Judah, and ye inhabitants of Jerusalem; Believe in the LORD your God, so shall ye be established; believe his prophets, so shall ye prosper." 2 Chronicles, 20:20.

"Believe His prophets, so shall ye prosper."

---

[1] If the reader has read books and heard sermons on 1888, saying that a few years after 1888 the message was finally accepted, read *The Return of the Latter Rain*, by Ron Duffield. Brother Duffield makes it all very clear.

[2] To learn more fully of the omega heresy, see *Omega Now* by this author. It's available at your favorite bookstore and on the Internet. Also in Kindle.

Chapter 11
Tidings Out of the East

Returning to our text above on Daniel 11:41, we should understand that the land and people of Israel must be spiritual, because the three nations of "Edom, Moab and the chief of the children of Ammon" have not existed for centuries. These nations were all relatives of Israel.[1] Today, they represent those who are not of Israel, but will join the church when the conflict heats up. They will "escape" out of the hand of the king of the north, the beast of Revelation, which is the Papacy. They will join spiritual Israel in the last great conflict. Although related to Israel, they were not a part of Israel. In Old Testament times, they could join with Israel after a time, if they chose to. We read in the *Seventh-day Adventist Bible Commentary*,

> "Edom: 'The descendents of Edom, or Esau, Jacob's older brother (Gen.36:1, 19). Because of this relationship, the Edomites were recognized by the Israelites as a brother nation, and the Mosaic law provided for their admission into the Hebrew nation in the 3rd generation, whereas Moabites and Amonites could not become full-fledged Israelites until the 10th generation (Deuteronomy 23:3-8).' "*The Seventh-day Adventist Bible Commentary*, Vol. 8, p. 303.

With this in mind, we should see that spiritual Edom, Moab and the Ammonites are those in the other churches who will join with God's people in the last days, when God's people are called out of Babylon. They correspond to the great multitude in Revelation 7:9. The "first fruits", the 144,000, are sealed from among God's people, modern Israel, and later the "great multitude" from all "nations and kindreds and peoples" will join with modern day Israel. They will be the harvest of the earth.[2]

11:42 **He shall stretch forth his hand also upon the countries: and the land of Egypt shall not escape.**

Tidings Out of the East

Egypt is Atheism,[2] and Atheism in any form, including Communism, will finally give way to the power of the Papacy. Rome has already shown her power and influence in the breaking up of the Soviet Union in 1989. Communism and the Papacy have long been enemies, but the Papacy will eventually prevail.

11:43 But he shall have power over the treasures of gold and of silver, and over all the precious things of Egypt: and the Libyans and the Ethiopians [shall be] at his steps.

No one knows the wealth of the Vatican Bank. It's secretive about what it holds under its umbrella, yet surely controls much, if not most, of the world's wealth. The Papacy will use this wealth to control the world, causing all to either accept the mark of the beast, or be banned from buying or selling.

We find this verse in Daniel to parallel the one in Revelation where John writes of the wealth of the great whore just before her destruction:

"And the kings of the earth, who have committed fornication and lived deliciously with her, shall bewail her, and lament for her, when they shall see the smoke of her burning, standing afar off for the fear of her torment, saying, Alas, alas that great city Babylon, that mighty city! For in one hour is thy judgment come. And the merchants of the earth shall weep and mourn over her; for no man buys their merchandise any more: The merchandise of gold, and silver, and precious stones, and of pearls . . . And the fruits that thy soul lusted after are departed from thee, and all things which were dainty and goodly are departed from thee, and thou shall find them no more at all. The merchants of these things, which were made rich by her, shall stand afar off for the fear of her torment, weeping and wailing, and saying, Alas, alas, that great city, that was clothed in fine linen, and purple, and scarlet, and decked with gold, and precious stones, and pearls! Revelation 18:9-16

11:44 But tidings out of the east and out of the north shall trouble him: therefore he shall go forth with great fury to destroy, and utterly to make away many.

In Daniel we have "tidings out of the east"; in Revelation 7:2 we have an "angel descending from the east." This angel in Revelation has "the seal of the living God" to seal the 144,000. In Daniel 11:44, the preaching of the good news of the sealing is here represented. The sealing hour message is the last message God's remnant church has for the world, and Satan will do all he can to prevent its spread. This is very good news and present truth, special truth for our time. Ellen White tells us:

> "Satan is now using every device in this sealing time to keep the minds of God's people from the present truth and to cause them to waver." *Early Writings*, 43.
>
> "There are many precious truths contained in the Word of God, but it is 'present truth' that the flock needs now. I have seen the danger of the messengers running off from the important points of present truth, to dwell upon subjects that are not calculated to unite the flock and sanctify the soul. Satan will here take every possible advantage to injure the cause." *Early Writings*, 63.

The rejection of this sealing truth is the omega of apostasy. When the sealing is better understood and more widely taught, Satan will use his earthy agents to accelerate the persecution of those who proclaim it, "to make away many." This parallels Revelation 12:17.[3]

The "tidings out of the east" refers to the renewed preaching of the sealing time message, the third angel's message of Revelation 14. In 1888, it wasn't properly understood, God's people failed at their post. It has been more than 120 years since that time, yet we're still here. We cry peace and safety, all is well. All is not good, we are still here. Today, there's increased emphasis on the sealing time message, but who will heed it?

If we want to unleash the power and anger of Satan, all we need to do is take the message of the final judgment and sealing and try to present it before others. Satan's followers don't want to hear it. Instead, they "rise up against it."[4]

Out of the East

What do we know about the direction east? A wind came out of the east to hold back the Red Sea.[5] An east wind blew on Jonah's head to where he fainted and wished to die.[6] A wind out of the east dried up Egypt to bring on the seven years of famine.[7]

Before the first coming of Jesus, a star came out of the east. Ellen White tells us this wasn't a star, but a band of angels.[8] Before Christ's second coming, an angel or messenger comes out of the east with the seal of God.[9]

This same sealing messenger of Revelation parallels the man with the writer's inkhorn in Ezekiel 9. He comes out of the "north" with the seal of God. This sealing is the good news. Five men with slaughter weapons come with him; they have the bad news. The news that will affect us depends on which side we stand on judgment day.

In Daniel 11:44, out of the east and north comes the "tidings" of God, the special blessing for today, the sealing time message. It's the final atonement, the cleansing of the sanctuary. Will we receive the seal of God or the mark of the beast? Will we be marked by the man with the writer's inkhorn, or be slaughtered by one who holds a destroying weapon?

> "And, behold, six men came from the way of the higher gate, which lieth toward the <u>north</u>, and every man a slaughter weapon in his hand; and one man among them [was] clothed with linen, with a writer's inkhorn by his side: and they went in, and stood beside the brazen altar." Ezekiel 9:2.

Those that accept the good news of the final judgment will take the message, cherish it and share it with the world. After the judgment concludes, the seven plagues will fall.

Notice in the verse below that after the plagues fall, there will be a searching for the Word of God. The seekers will be looking in vain to the "north even to the east." The prophet tells us,

> "These plagues are not universal, or the inhabitants of the earth would be wholly cut off. Yet they will be the most awful scourges that have ever been known to mortals. All the judgments upon men, prior to the close of probation, have been mingled with mercy. The pleading blood of Christ has shielded the sinner from receiving the full measure of his guilt; but in the final judgment, wrath is poured out unmixed with mercy.
>
> "In that day, multitudes will desire the shelter of God's mercy which they have so long despised. 'Behold, the days come, saith the Lord God, that I will send a famine in the land, not a famine of bread, nor a thirst for water, but of hearing the words of the Lord: and they shall wander from sea to sea, and from the <u>north even to the east</u>, they shall run to and fro to seek the word of the Lord, and shall not find it.' Amos 8:11, 12." *Great Controversy*, 628,9.

Planting His Tabernacle

11:45 And he shall plant the tabernacles of his palace between the seas in the glorious holy mountain; yet he shall come to his end, and none shall help him.

"Thy way, O God, [is] in the sanctuary: who [is so] great a God as [our] God?" Psalms 77:13. God communed with His people in the wilderness in the sanctuary, then later in Solomon's temple. He teaches us the plan of salvation with the sanctuary motif. If we need to know His plan of salvation, we must look to His teachings on the sanctuary.

That being the case, to deceive us theologically, Satan will need to do away with the sanctuary or pervert it, twist it or in some way misrepresent it. For years, the Papacy has placed its way of salvation in the place of God's way. Priests for centuries have placed themselves between our High Priest and humanity, but in the last days, Rome will do more.

Since present truth is what we need, Satan must place his counterfeit in its place. This is undoubtedly a perversion of the same message. Ultimately, it will climax in the Sunday Law, requiring the honoring of the first day of the week. Satan places his "tabernacle" or sanctuary between the seas and the holy mountain. That is, he plants his sanctuary error between the people, "the seas,"5 and the temple of God in the holy mountain, the city of God. New Jerusalem is now in heaven, where God's temple stands today. Christ, our high priest, is ready to pass on to us the blessings of the judgment. But do we see it or is our vision blocked by Satan obstructing our view? Yes, Satan blocks our vision to the understanding of the true sanctuary teaching, which is the third angel's message. The people of God in His church today, who are falling for this deception, are falling victim to the omega.

"None Shall Help Him"

In Daniel 11:45 it says, "And none shall help him." Daniel 8 parallels this verse where it says, ". . . he shall be broken without hand." Daniel 8:25. This verse in Daniel 8, "broken without hand", ends the reign of the little horn of Daniel 8. Daniel 11:45 says, "none shall help him", ending the reign of the king of the north here in Daniel 11. In both cases, we are dealing with the Papacy.

We must remember the message of Daniel 11 concerning the king of the north is not a doctrine just to be added to our list of doctrines for doctrine's sake. Instead, it's about the sealing of the people of God. Mere knowledge alone is not the goal here, but it's the sealing of God's people that we need. The blessing is for modern-day Israel (144,000) and the children of Edom Moab and Ammon (the great multitude).

Accepting the message "out of the east", the tidings of the last day message, the seal of the living God should be our goal. Knowledge cannot save us, but we can be lost for the lack of it.

"My people are destroyed for lack of knowledge: because thou hast rejected knowledge, I will also reject thee." Hosea 4:6.

"Not For Thy Righteousness"

Has the Seventh-day Adventist Church been faithful? Do we know all that we should? Are we on the path to what God has in store for us? How close are we to entering the Promised Land? Paul tells us,

Tidings Out of the East

"Moreover, brethren, I would not that ye should be ignorant, how that all our fathers were under the cloud, and all passed through the sea; . . .Now all these things happened unto them for ensamples: and they are written for our admonition, upon whom the ends of the world are come." 1 Corinthians 10:1, 11.

Did the Israelites in Moses' day go into the Promised Land because they finally got it right? If the events on the journey of the Israelites from Egypt to Canaan are an example to us "upon whom the ends of the world are come", then we should find out what it was that finally made it possible for the Israelites to enter Canaan. They finally entered after forty years of wandering, and did so even with a lack of faith. The Scriptures tell us this,

"Understand therefore this day, that the LORD thy God [is] he which goeth over before thee; [as] a consuming fire he shall destroy them, and he shall bring them down before thy face: so shalt thou drive them out, and destroy them quickly, as the LORD hath said unto thee.
"Speak not thou in thine heart, after that the LORD thy God hath cast them out from before thee, saying, For my righteousness the LORD hath brought me in to possess this land: but for the wickedness of these nations the LORD doth drive them out from before thee.
"Not for thy righteousness, or for the uprightness of thine heart, dost thou go to possess their land: but for the wickedness of these nations the LORD thy God doth drive them out from before thee, and that he may perform the word which the LORD sware unto thy fathers, Abraham, Isaac, and Jacob.
"Understand therefore, that the LORD thy God giveth thee not this good land to possess it for thy righteousness; for thou [art] a stiffnecked people." Deuteronomy 9:3-6.

Today, we have more than a lack of faith; we also have the omega, which will lead to the shaking. Within Laodicea, "many shall be overthrown." Daniel 11:41.

----

[1] Genesis 19:36-38

[2] *The Great Controversy*, 269

[3] "And the dragon was wroth with the woman, and went to make war with the remnant of her seed, which keep the commandments of God, and have the testimony of Jesus Christ." Revelation 12:17

[4] *Early Writings*, 271

[5] Exodus 14:21

[6] Jonah 4:8

[7] Genesis 41:27

[8] Desire of Ages, 60

[9] Revelation 7:2

[10] Revelation 14:14-16

Chapter 12
Michael Stands Up

As we have studied, the last verse of Daniel 11 ends with the national Sunday law and the sealing. Before that, tidings come from the east; it's the truth on the seal of the living God, the judgment hour message, and as we will see later, it's the latter rain. The time of trouble comes after the sealing, followed by the second coming. Ellen White confirms this sequence of events,

"Just before we entered it [the time of trouble], we all received the seal of the living God. Then I saw the four angels cease to hold the four winds. And I saw famine, pestilence and sword, nation rose against nation, and the whole world was in confusion.--*SDA Bible Commentary*, vol. 7, 968 (1846).

"I saw angels hurrying to and fro in heaven. An angel with a writer's inkhorn by his side returned from the earth and reported to Jesus that his work was done, and the saints were numbered and sealed. Then I saw Jesus, who had been ministering before the ark containing the ten commandments, throw down the censer. He raised His hands, and with a loud voice said, "It is done."--*Early Writings*, 279 (1858).

"An angel returning from the earth announces that his work is done; the final test has been brought upon the world, and all who have proved themselves loyal to the divine precepts have received "the seal of the living God." Then Jesus ceases His intercession in the sanctuary above. He lifts His hands, and with a loud voice says, "It is done."--*Great Controversy*, 613 (1911).

Michael Stands Up

The first verse of Daniel 12 tells us about the time of trouble when Michael "stands up." At this time, He has thrown down the censor, for the judgment is finished. The Saints have been sealed; the time of trouble is next.

12:1 And at that time shall Michael stand up, the great prince which stands for the children of thy people: and there shall be a time of trouble, such as never was since there was a nation [even] to that same time: and at that time thy people shall be delivered, every one that shall be found written in the book.

Michael means, "One who is like God." This is the King of God's people, because He "stands up" to take command of the world as did the earlier kings of Persian, Greece and Rome.[1] Jesus standing up and taking over as the king corresponds to Revelation where the seventh angel sounds:

"And the seventh angel sounded; and there were great voices in heaven, saying, The kingdoms of this world are become [the kingdoms] of our Lord, and of his Christ; and he shall reign forever and ever." Revelation 11:15

The Mystery of God is Finished

Christ receives the "kingdoms of this world," in Revelation 10:15, which occurs when the seventh angels sounds his trumpet. However, we need to see that just before the angel sounds announcing Jesus as our king, the mystery of God is finished.[2]

"But in the days of the voice of the seventh angel, when he shall <u>begin to sound</u>, the mystery of God should be finished, as he hath declared to his servants the prophets." Revelation 10:7. KJV

A better translation than "begins to sound" is "about to sound." So, the mystery of God is finished just as the seventh angel is "about to sound." The KJV translates it, "begins to sound", but if we check other versions, we will find the finishing of the mystery of God is just immediately before the sounding of the seventh trumpet. For example, the NIV says,

"But in the days when the seventh angel is <u>about to sound</u> his trumpet, the mystery of God will be accomplished, just as he announced to his servants the prophets." Revelation 10:7, NIV.

The mystery of God is "Christ in you." Colossians 1:27. This is the New Covenant promise fulfilled and finalized. Jeremiah tells us of this promise,

"Behold, the days come, says the LORD, that I will make a new covenant with the house of Israel, and with the house of Judah: Not according to the covenant that I made with their fathers in the day [that] I took them by the hand to bring them out of the land of Egypt; which my covenant they brake, although I was an husband unto them, says the LORD: But this [shall be] the covenant that I will make with the house of Israel; After those days, says the LORD, I will put my law in their inward parts, and write it in their hearts; and will be their God, and they shall be my people. And they shall teach no more every man his neighbor, and every man his brother, saying, Know the LORD: for they shall all know me, from the least of them unto the greatest of them, says the LORD: for I will forgive their iniquity, and I will remember their sin no more." Jeremiah 31-31-34.

This is the final atonement, the investigative judgment, the Day of Atonement, Yom Kippur. It's the sealing of God's people. After God's people are sealed, the "time of trouble" commences.

The Time of Trouble

Ellen White tells us about the sealing and what happens after it's completed. First, the work of Christ is finished, and then the seven last plagues come in the time called Jacob's trouble,

> "I saw that the four angels would hold the four winds until Jesus' work was done in the sanctuary, and then will come the seven last plagues. . . This was the time of Jacob's trouble." *Early Writings*, p. 36, 37.

After His work as our High Priest, Jesus will take off his priestly robes and put on his kingly garments to come to gather His sealed from the earth. In between those times, God's sealed saints will be tested in the time of trouble.

> "I also saw that many do not realize what they must be in order to live in the sight of the Lord <u>without a high priest in the sanctuary</u> through the <u>time of trouble</u>. Those who receive the seal of the living God and are protected in the time of trouble <u>must reflect the image of Jesus fully</u>." *Early Writings*, p. 71. Underline supplied.

> "Says the prophet: 'Who may abide the day of His coming? and who shall stand when He appeareth? for He is like a refiner's fire, and like fullers' soap: and He shall sit as a refiner and purifier of silver: and He shall purify the sons of Levi, and purge them as gold and silver, that they may offer unto the Lord an offering in righteousness.' Malachi 3:2, 3. <u>Those who are living upon the earth when the intercession of Christ shall cease in the sanctuary above are to stand in the sight of a holy God without a mediator.</u> Their robes must be spotless, their characters must be purified from sin by the blood of sprinkling. Through the grace of God and their own diligent effort they must be conquerors in the battle with evil. While the investigative judgment is going forward in heaven, while the sins of penitent believers are being removed from the sanctuary, there is to be a special work of purification, of putting away of sin, among God's people upon earth. This work is more clearly presented in the messages of Revelation 14." *Great Controversy*, p. 425. Underline supplied.

Some balk at this statement, saying there will indeed be a mediator in the sanctuary; they say, God will never leave us. True, He's with us always, but not as a mediator, not as our high priest. Through the time of trouble, God will be with us in the person of the Holy Spirit and will never leave us. God was with Adam and Eve before their fall; however, He was not with them as a mediator. Only sinners need a mediator, not those perfected through the blood of Christ. This perfecting work is the work of the Day of Atonement, the cleansing of the sanctuary. Leviticus tells us about the Day of Atonement,

> "For on that day shall [the priest] make an atonement for you, to cleanse you, [that] ye may be clean from all your sins before the LORD." Leviticus 16:30.

Ellen White tells us that the final atonement, the investigative judgment, is the time when the new covenant promise will be fulfilled,

> "Thus will be realized the complete fulfillment of the new-covenant promise: 'I will forgive their iniquity, and I will remember their sin no more.' 'In those days, and in that time, saith the Lord, <u>the iniquity of Israel shall be sought for, and there shall be none; and the sins of Judah, and they shall not be found</u>.' Jeremiah 31:34; 50:20. 'In that day shall the branch of the Lord be beautiful and glorious, and the fruit of the earth shall be excellent and comely for them that are escaped of Israel. And it shall come to pass, that he that is left in Zion, and he that remaineth in Jerusalem, shall be called holy, even everyone that is written among the living in Jerusalem.' Isaiah 4:2, 3.
>
> "The work of <u>the investigative judgment</u> and the blotting out of sins is to be accomplished before the second advent of the Lord. . . . When the investigative judgment closes, Christ will come, and His reward will be with Him to give to every man as his work shall be." *Great Controversy*, p. 485. Underlining supplied.

The First Resurrection

The resurrection of the righteous comes after the saints are sealed with the latter rain and pass through the time of Jacob's trouble. Daniel tells us,

12:2 And many of them that sleep in the dust of the earth shall awake, some to everlasting life, and some to shame [and] everlasting contempt.

This resurrection is not of the wicked in general; they come forth after the millennium.[3] This awakening of the dead includes two groups, those who are righteous and the wicked that were present during Christ's final days on earth. They mocked Him and derided Him as He hung there suffering for them. Along with the general resurrection of God's sleeping saints, this is a special resurrection for those who were responsibly for Jesus to be on the cross and for those who mistreated Him. Revelation confirms this, "Behold, he comes with clouds; and every eye shall see him, and they [also] which pierced him:" Revelation 1:7.[4]

Michael Stands Up - 12

12:3 And they that be wise shall shine as the brightness of the firmament; and they that turn many to righteousness as the stars forever and ever.

What was lost in Eden, at this time, will be completely restored. What was lost? Justification, sanctification and glorification were no longer a part of the lives of Adam and Eve after their sin. They could no longer stand before God and expect His acceptance. They could no longer continue alive eternally, because the "wages of sin is death." Only with a life without sin could they live forever.

This sinful condition was passed on down the line, coming even to our time. Today, we need to be found just before God. Not only do we need to be forgiven, we also need to have all sin removed from our lives. Otherwise, we can never enter into eternal life. No sin or sinner will enter heaven. Finally, our bodies must be changed and will be, when Jesus comes.

At the end of the vision, here in Daniel 12:3, we have the saints of God shining forth as "righteousness as the stars." They have received the final atonement. The righteous dead are resurrected and the righteous living are translated when Jesus comes. They are restored. Now the King can also be restored as king, restored to His restored kingdom with its perfectly restored people. They will be living among the restored temple, a reminder of what God has done for them in Jesus Christ

---

[1] Daniel 8:22,23,25; 11:2-4,7,14:20-21.)

[2] You might have noticed that between the time the mystery of God is finished (Revelation 10:7) and the time the seventh angel sounds (Revelation 11:15) there are 18 verses. If one event follows the other so closely, then why is there so much text in between.
In these 18 verses of Revelation from 10:7 to 11:15, John is telling us where we are in world history, first with the "little book" and then with the French Revolution. The "little book" is the book of Daniel, which was opened at the "time of the end" in 1798, at the end of the 1260 years. The "little book" tells us of the upcoming cleansing of the sanctuary in Daniel 8:14, the judgment that started in 1844. This judgment will be realized in the Sunday law, and the sealing.
The French Revolution was very close to the same time. In fact, the end of the 1260 years came about because the French took the pope captive in 1798. The book of Revelation is introducing us to the king of the south of Daniel 11:40, "spiritually called Sodom and Egypt," Atheism.

[3] Revelation 20:5

[4] See also *The Great Controversy*, 637

Tidings Out of the East

The Shaking

The chapter on the shaking in *Early Writings* is very important. Here are some of the high points,

"I saw some, with strong faith and agonizing cries, pleading with God. Their countenances were pale and marked with deep anxiety, expressive of their internal struggle. . .

"Evil angels crowded around, pressing darkness upon them to shut out Jesus from their view, that their eyes might be drawn to the darkness that surrounded them, and thus they be led to distrust God and murmur against Him. Their only safety was in keeping their eyes directed upward. . . Some, I saw, did not participate in this work of agonizing and pleading. They seemed indifferent and careless. They were not resisting the darkness around them, and it shut them in like a thick cloud. . . . I asked the meaning of the shaking I had seen and was shown that it would be caused by the straight testimony called forth by the counsel of the True Witness to the Laodiceans. This will have its effect upon the heart of the receiver, and will lead him to exalt the standard and pour forth the straight truth. Some will not bear this straight testimony. They will rise up against it, and this is what will cause a shaking among God's people.

"I saw that the testimony of the True Witness has not been half heeded. The solemn testimony upon which the destiny of the church hangs has been lightly esteemed, if not entirely disregarded. . . . Said the angel, "Look ye!" My attention was then turned to the company I had seen, who were mightily shaken. I was shown those whom I had before seen weeping and praying in agony of spirit. . . .

"The numbers of this company had lessened. Some had been shaken out and left by the way. The careless and indifferent, who did not join with those who prized victory and salvation enough to perseveringly plead and agonize for it, did not obtain it, and they were left behind in darkness, and their places were immediately filled by others taking hold of the truth and coming into the ranks. Evil angels still pressed around them, but could have no power over them.

"I heard those clothed with the armor speak forth the truth with great power. It had effect. Many had been bound; some wives by their husbands, and some children by their parents. The honest who had been prevented from hearing the truth now eagerly laid hold upon it. All fear of their relatives was gone, and the truth alone was exalted to them. They had been hungering and thirsting for truth; it was dearer and more precious than life. I asked what had made this great change. An angel answered, "It is the latter rain, the refreshing from the presence of the Lord, the loud cry of the third angel." . . .

"Soon I heard the voice of God, which shook the heavens and the earth. There was a mighty earthquake. Buildings were shaken down on every side. I then heard a triumphant shout of victory, loud, musical, and clear. I looked upon the company, who, a short time before, were in such distress and bondage. Their captivity was turned. A glorious light shone upon them. How beautiful they then looked!" *Early Writings* 269-273.

www.Latter-Rain-Project.com

Chapter 13
"Shut up the Words"

Following here in Daniel 12, we have three time lines we must deal with. Using the day for a year principle, we have 1260 years, 1290 years and 1335 years. However, these years must be sealed up for a time before they will be understood. Daniel is told that at the "time of the end" they would be unsealed. According to Ellen White, the unsealing of the book of Daniel was in 1798.

> "No such message [on the judgment] has ever been given in past ages. Paul, as we have seen, did not preach it; he pointed his brethren into the then far-distant future for the coming of the Lord. The Reformers did not proclaim it. Martin Luther placed the judgment about three hundred years in the future from his day. <u>But since 1798 the book of Daniel has been unsealed, knowledge of the prophecies has increased, and many have proclaimed the solemn message of the judgment near.</u>" *Great Controversy*, 356. Underlining supplied.

In the following verse, we see that Daniel's book is unsealed at the "time of the end." Therefore, if Daniel's book is unsealed in 1798, according to Ellen White, and Daniel's book is unsealed at the "time of the end," according to Daniel, then 1798 is the "time of the end."

12:4 But thou, O Daniel, shut up the words, and seal the book, [even] to the time of the end: many shall run to and fro, and knowledge shall be increased.

Two men, probably angels, appeared to Daniel, one on each side of the Tigris River. They seemed to be interested in the future of God's people and wanted to know what the three prophetic time lines meant. One asked Jesus, "how long."

12:5 Then I Daniel looked, and, behold, there stood other two, the one on this side of the bank of the river, and the other on that side of the bank of the river.

12:6 And [one] said to the man clothed in linen, which [was] upon the waters of the river, How long [shall it be to] the end of these wonders?

Some expositors have placed these three time lines at the end of the world, around the close of probation or later. So, how do we know these periods are before 1844 as they were interpreted by the Millerites before 1844?

One clue is that the angel raised his right hand and swore in the name of God that there would be "a time, times and a half." That is to say, there is a prophetic time line meant here. However, in Revelation 10:6 the angel holding the "little book" raised his right hand and in the name of God swore there "should be time no longer."

This is the time between the beginning of the "time of the end," From 1798 to 1844. It's the time the "little book" was opened, the book of Daniel, which tells of the judgment, starting in 1844. The angel in Daniel 12 must be talking about the time before 1844, because after 1844, there is no more "tracing of the prophetic time." Ellen White tells us,

> "This is represented by the angel standing with one foot on the sea, proclaiming with a most solemn oath that time should be no longer.
> "This time, which the angel declares with a solemn oath, is not the end of this world's history, neither of probationary time, but of prophetic time, which should precede the advent of our Lord. That is, the people will not have another message upon definite time. <u>After this period of time, reaching from 1842 to 1844, there can be no definite tracing of the prophetic time</u>. The longest reckoning reaches to the autumn of 1844." 7 *SDA Bible Commentary*, p. 971. Underlining supplied.

In summary, the 1260, 1290 and 1335 years must be before 1844, at which time the prophecies concerning time ended.

1260 Years

The first time line mentioned is the 1260 years, from 538 to 1798. Every Seventh-day Adventists should know and understand this time line very well. It shows up in both Daniel and Revelation. This 1260-year period holds together and supports the repeat and expand key. It provides a common anchor point in the several prophecies in which it appears.

During the 1260 years, the papacy controlled the European scene. Here in Daniel the "power of the holy people" was scattered. In Revelation, the woman, the holy people, were in the wilderness for a "time, times and half a time." Revelation 12:14. Daniel's text follows,

"Shut up the Words" - 13

12:7 And I heard the man clothed in linen, which [was] upon the waters of the river, when he held up his right hand and his left hand unto heaven, and sware by him that liveth for ever that [it shall be] for a time, times, and an half; and when he shall have accomplished to scatter the power of the holy people, all these [things] shall be finished.

There's nothing new here, shortly before 1843 Josiah Litch drew up a chart dealing with these periods. Ellen White tells us about the validity of this chart:

"I have seen that the 1843 chart was directed by the hand of the Lord, and that it should not be altered; that the figures were as He wanted them; that His hand was over and hid a mistake in some of the figures, so that none could see it, until His hand was removed." *Early Writings*, p. 74.

The chart contained these three periods of time, as well as the 2300 days of Daniel 8:14. We know the 2300 days were correct in their starting and ending points, but not in the meaning of the cleansing of the sanctuary. The 1260 extended from A.D. 538 when the Little Horn "subdued" the last of the three horns (Daniel 7:24) and extended to 1798, when the pope of Rome, the little horn, was taken captive by the French army.

1290 Years

On Litch's chart, the 1290 years started in 508 when Clovis, King of the Franks, set up the priesthood of the Roman Catholic Church, effectively taking away the daily or continual mediation of Christ in the heavenly sanctuary. [1]

Of course, he can't take away the true "daily" with Christ in heaven, but the effect was to take it away from the minds of the believers, setting up a false "daily" which is the system of priests taking the place of Christ in the eyes of the people. In place of the true, the Roman church set up the "abomination that makes desolate," that is, she placed a mere man between Christ and mankind, creating an earthly priesthood, replacing Divinity with humanity. Also about this time, obedience to the seventh-day Sabbath was transferred to the Pagan day of worship, Sunday. The 1290 time line ended in 1798.

12:8 And I heard, but I understood not: then said I, O my Lord, what [shall be] the end of these [things]?

Because Daniel didn't want the vision to continue far into the Christian era, even to 1844, maybe he just refused to believe his ears.

Tidings Out of the East

He was sure he was misunderstanding, because he just couldn't accept a 2300 years prophecy.

12:9 And he said, Go thy way, Daniel: for the words [are] closed up and sealed till the time of the end.
12:10 Many shall be purified, and made white, and tried; but the wicked shall do wickedly: and none of the wicked shall understand; but the wise shall understand.
12:11 And from the time [that] the daily [sacrifice] shall be taken away, and the abomination that makes desolate set up, [there shall be] a thousand two hundred and ninety days.

The word "sacrifice" is a supplied word. The word "daily" means the continual. This daily or continual is the daily ministration of Jesus as our High Priest in the heavenly sanctuary.[1] Jesus started this mediation when He ascended into heaven. The daily ministry was in effect "taken away" when Clovis set up a false, abominable priesthood. It lasted until 1798 when the Papacy received its deadly wound, the pope being cast into prison by the French.

1335 Years

Finally, the third time line of 1335 years is said to start in 508 and end 1335 years later in 1843. In that year, there was great excitement about the second coming of Jesus. People repented of their sins and grew in faith, in expectation of an event that failed to materialize. Near the fall of that year, it was discovered that a mistake had been made in the calculation. It was incorrect by one year because a year zero had been added to the calculation, causing the calculation to end in 1843. Taking away the year zero moved the date back one more year to 1844, and rightfully so.

12:12 Blessed [is] he that waits, and comes to the thousand three hundred and five and thirty days.

The dates of the 1335 days are explained above. Although greatly disappointed when Jesus didn't appear as hoped, the saints are called "blessed" because of the joyous experience they went through. In addition, now they can receive the latter rain in the final atonement, made possible by Christ who has entered the most holy place of the heavenly sanctuary. The judgment is good news, and all Christians should be looking forward to it. However, they will only do so, if they

"Shut up the Words" - 13

have the correct understanding of what it will do for them. In short, it prepares God's people for the second coming.

The book of Daniel, a book of judgment, was to be understood "at the end of the days."

12:13 But go thou thy way till the end [be]: for thou shall rest, and stand in thy lot at the end of the days.

Daniel will stand in his place at the end of the days, at the end of the world, starting around 1798 when his prophecies would be more clearly studied and understood. Daniel wrote for our time. Though he is in his grave, he is alive in the minds and hearts of many. Today, his words are unsealed.

---

[1] The verse in question is this,
"**And from the time [that] the daily [sacrifice] shall be taken away, and the abomination that makes desolate set up, [there shall be] a thousand two hundred and ninety days. Daniel 12:11.**"
This is referring back to the same event spoken of earlier in Daniel 11, where it says,
"**And arms shall stand on his part, and they shall pollute the sanctuary of strength, and shall take away the daily [sacrifice], and they shall place the abomination that makes desolate." Daniel 11:31.**
These are the same event. In Daniel 12, the event is mentioned to begin the 1290 years from 508 to 1798. In Daniel 11, it's the actual event occurring in history in 508. In both places, we have the "daily" and the "abomination that makes desolate."
By some authors, the "daily" is interpreted as "Paganism." However, does Paganism fit here? How is Paganism 'taken away?" One expositor says the word here really means to establish, but he is using the work translated "taken away" in an earlier verse, Daniel 8:11. This is a different Hebrew word with Strong's number H7311. It has the meaning of *to exalt, raise up*, or *lift up*, a more positive meaning than to "take away."
Paganism is a possibility in Daniel 8:11. It might be Paganism in this verse for "daily,' meaning to exalt Paganism as the Roman Church *lifted up* Paganism when it absorbed most of its ideas into Christianity, corrupting the truth. In a sense, Paganism was lifted up while Christianity was put down.
However, in Daniel 11 and 12 Strong's number is H5493. It's used for "taken away," meaning to *take away* or *remove*. In both of the two above verses, we have the daily *taken away*. In its place, the *abomination of desolation* is *set up*. Logic tells us that what is taken away must be similar to what is set up; one thing is exchanged for something else.
The proponents of the word *daily* being Paganism say that Paganism was taken away and apostate Romanism was set up. This has to be the replacing of either something good for something bad or something bad for something good. However, how was Paganism taken away? It wasn't. Instead, it was established within the Christian Church, making it an abominable thing. Ellen White tells us that when the

Tidings Out of the East

idolatrous standards of Rome in A.D. 70 stood just outside the gates of Jerusalem, that counted as being the abomination of desolation. Here is what she says,

"And the Saviour warned His followers: "When ye therefore shall see the abomination of desolation, spoken of by Daniel the prophet, stand in the holy place, . . . then let them which be in Judea flee into the mountains." Matthew 24:15, 16; Luke 21:20, 21. When the idolatrous standards of the Romans should be set up in the holy ground, which extended some furlongs outside the city walls, then the followers of Christ were to find safety in flight." *Great Controversy*, 26.

The abomination that makes desolate here is allowing the gods of Rome to enter the sanctuary. They entered the earthy sanctuary and later destroyed the temple. This actually took away the daily sacrifice in the earthly temple, because there was no more temple in which to do any sacrificing. It was more symbolic than actual, because Priest Jesus already was at that time in Heaven in the sanctuary there. Jesus was the Lamb to which all those slain animals had pointed. At this time, A.D.70, the daily had been taken away (no more sacrifices were possible) and the abomination was set up (the Roman standards had polluted the sanctuary by their presence.)

Doesn't it follow, that later in the time of Clovis and Constantine, the Roman church took God or something that represents or teaches of God out of the Sanctuary, replacing it with Roman gods, or teachings or practices? Of course, no earthly power is going to be able to take God from His temple in heaven, but effectively this can happen in teaching or practice. In Daniel 8, it says this about the little horn, the Papacy,

"And an host was given [him] against the daily [sacrifice] by reason of transgression, and it cast down the truth to the ground; and it practiced, and prospered." Daniel 8:12.

As for whether the "daily" is Paganism or the daily ministration of Christ as our high priest, the result is the same. Satan took the truth and replaced it with error. This error continued through the time of Papal suppression of the truth, 538-1798. Satan through the Papacy kept the truth of justification by faith alone from the eyes of the on-looking masses. It disfigured the character of God to the point that the sentiment that God is love was almost entirely disbelieved. Very few survived the onslaught of Papal lies and misrepresentations.

Satan through a Christian façade of Paganism causes the "abomination that makes desolate" by absorbing Paganism into the Roman Church. He did it by keeping the truth from the eyes of humanity, by "casting the truth to the ground," while he "practiced and prospered." We can choose one side of this debate or the other or neither, but no matter which side we choose, Paganism as the "daily" or the ministry of Christ in the sanctuary as the "daily", we need to know what's happening today. If we deal too much with this controversy, we might miss the real message God has for us.

Chapter 14
The Latter Rain

The cleansing of the sanctuary of Daniel 8:14 is more than a doctrine for doctrine's sake; it's not just for the prospective church member to be studied only until baptism. No, it's the final atonement, typified in the Day of Atonement at the end of the Jewish ceremonial year. It was the final act of cleansing, known as Yom Kippur, occurring just before the Feast of Tabernacles, which typifies the millennium. Moses tells us in Leviticus 16 what is to be cleansed. It's good news, and we should be eagerly awaiting it.

"For on that day shall [the priest] make an atonement for you, to cleanse you, [that] ye may be clean from all your sins before the LORD." Leviticus 16:30.

Daniel 7 parallels Daniel 8, showing that the judgment of Daniel 7:25 is the cleansing of the sanctuary in Daniel 8:14. The "tidings out of the east" of Daniel 11:44 parallels the judgment of Daniel 7 and 8. In Revelation, we find the mark of the beast is decreed in opposition to the seal of the Living God coming from the east.[1]

With this in mind, we need to ask ourselves why this sealing, cleansing work has not occurred and why we're still on this earth. It's been more than 160 years after the judgment of the living was to commence sometime soon after 1844. What have we been doing wrong? What is it that has been keeping God's people from the final act of cleansing?

This cleansing is brought to us in the form of the latter rain.

"Then shall we know, [if] we follow on to know the LORD: his going forth is prepared as the morning; and he shall come unto us as the rain, as the latter [and] former rain unto the earth." Hosea 6: 3.

Question: What does the latter rain do in the lives of God's people? In *Testimonies to Minister*, in the chapter called "Pray for the

Tidings Out of the East

Latter Rain" we find the answer. The study of this chapter should leave the reader with a clear understanding of the work of the latter rain. Some teach we will have to be perfect, without any sin, even before the latter rain falls. Ellen White makes statements that seem to say just that. However, after reading the chapter in *Testimonies to Ministers*, which was written specifically for our understanding of the latter rain, we should have no doubts remaining.

Other Questions

Have you received the latter rain? How do we receive it and when? Is it now falling? Could we have missed it, or is it yet in the future? How do we know when it falls? All these important questions have been and still are being asked, and we must know the answers. Nevertheless, the most important question at this time is, does the latter rain make a change in the behavior or character of the people of God? Will God's people be living totally and completely without sin before the latter rain falls, or can we expect a change in the character as a blessing of the refreshing showers?

The Symbolism Defined

As mentioned above, *Testimonies to Ministers* devotes one entire chapter to the latter rain. The name of the chapter is "Pray for the Latter Rain." Much of this chapter will be covered in this presentation. Here is the beginning of what Ellen White says:

> "In the East the former rain falls at the sowing time. It is necessary in order that the seed may germinate. Under the influence of the fertilizing showers, the tender shoot springs up. The latter rain, falling near the close of the season, ripens the grain and prepares it for the sickle. The Lord employs these operations of nature to represent the work of the Holy Spirit. As the dew and the rain are given first to cause the seed to germinate, and then to ripen the harvest, so the Holy Spirit is given to carry forward, from one stage to another, the PROCESS OF SPIRITUAL GROWTH. The ripening of the grain represents the completion of THE WORK OF GOD'S GRACE IN THE SOUL. By the power of the Holy Spirit THE MORAL IMAGE OF GOD IS TO BE PERFECTED IN THE CHARACTER. We are to be wholly transformed into the likeness of Christ." *Testimonies to Ministers*, 506. Capitalization supplied.

The symbolism of the former and latter rain is simple. The former rain is given at the beginning of the planting season to start the growing process. The latter rain is needed before the harvest to bring the crops to total maturity (perfection) for the reaper's sickle. God has used this illustration to show us how he gives His people the character and power to overcome sin through the gift of the Holy Spirit.

The Latter Rain - 14

When a sinner first accepts Christ as his Savior, he receives the Holy Spirit in the form of the former rain. As he progresses in Christian growth over the period of his lifetime, he continues to be refreshed by the spirit as symbolized by the early or former rain.

However, there's a time in earth's history when God will pour out a special blessing on His people in the form of the latter rain. For this blessing, the people of God should be eagerly awaiting. To be perfect by being "wholly transformed into the image of Christ" should be our constant goal. God has made it possible in these last days in the gift of the latter rain, the outpouring of His Spirit upon all His faithful people.

That Important Question Again

Does the latter rain bring about any change in our characters? That is, are we changed spiritually by the latter rain? Is there spiritual growth under the latter rain?

Most historic Seventh-day Adventists teach that the latter rain will fall only on those who have become perfect, totally without sin. They say the latter rain brings no change in the spiritual condition of the believer. In other words, there's no spiritual growth, no character change, under the latter rain.

Let's review what the messenger of the Lord said in the above: quotation in the chapter, "Pray for the Latter Rain."

1. "The latter rain, falls near the close of the season, ripens the grain and prepares it for the sickle." This perfecting of the image of God in man will be by the power of the Holy Spirit. It's illustrated as the ripening of the harvest.

2. Under the latter rain, we will be "transformed into likeness of Christ. . . The moral image is to be perfected in the character."

3. The latter rain is a "completion of the work of God's grace in the soul."

In no way does this indicate we must be without sin before the latter rain falls. It doesn't say the latter rain will fall only on those people who have been made faultless with no remaining sins to be revealed or in any way yet have sins to be dealt with. It doesn't say all unknown sins will have all been made known and overcome before the showers of refreshing can fall. Instead, it's very clear that the latter rain *does* bring about a change in the spiritual condition of God's people.

Again, in the following quotation we find that "spiritual grace" will be given to "God's church," both in the former and in the latter rains.

> "It is true that in the time of the end, when God's work in the earth is closing, the earnest efforts put forth by consecrated believers under the guidance of the Holy Spirit are to be accompanied by special tokens of divine favor. Under the figure of the early and the latter rain, that falls in Eastern lands at seedtime and harvest, the Hebrew prophets foretold the bestowal of <u>spiritual grace</u> in extraordinary measure upon God's church. The outpouring of the Spirit in the days of the apostles was the beginning of the early, or former, rain, and glorious was the result. To the end of time the presence of the Spirit is to abide with the true church." *Acts of the Apostles,* 54, 55. Underlining supplied.

We Must Not Wait

To some, this might seem like a license to freely sin and wait until the time of the latter rain, when all sins will be completely and perfectly blotted out. Satan would love us to take this stand as many have, leaving off until later what needs to be done now. This attitude is a selfish solution that cares not for trying to overcome nor to give glory to God by obedience. It's not only selfish to neglect the present work as symbolized by the former rain, but very dangerous as well. The last-day prophet writes,

> "Many have in a great measure failed to receive the former rain. They have not obtained all the benefits that God has thus provided for them. They expect that the lack will be supplied by the latter rain. When the <u>*richest abundance of grace*</u> shall be bestowed, they intend to open their hearts to receive it. They are making a terrible mistake. The work that God has begun in *the human heart* in giving His light and knowledge must be continually going forward. Every individual must realize his own necessity. The heart must be emptied of every defilement and cleansed for the indwelling of the Spirit. It was by the confession and forsaking of sin, by earnest prayer and consecration of themselves to God, that the early disciples prepared for the outpouring of the Holy Spirit on the Day of Pentecost. The same work, only in greater degree, must be done now. Then the human agent had only to ask for the blessing, and wait for the Lord to perfect the work concerning him. It is God who began the work, and <u>*He will finish His work, making man complete in Jesus Christ.*</u> But there must be no neglect of the grace represented by the former rain. Only those who are <u>living up to the light they have</u> will receive greater light." *Testimonies to Ministers,* 507. Emphasis supplied.

The latter rain is called the "richest abundance of grace" and "spiritual grace." (Acts of the Apostles, 55.) It's the "richest" that will ever be bestowed, but the former rain must first be received. God's people must be "living up to the light they have", and as stated below, "daily advancing in the exemplification of the active Christian virtues."

If not, they won't receive the perfecting latter rain or even know when it's falling around them:

> "Unless we are <u>daily advancing in the exemplification of the active Christian virtues</u>, we shall not recognize the manifestations of the Holy Spirit in the latter rain. It may be falling on hearts all around us, but we shall not discern or receive it." *Testimonies to Ministers,* 507. Underlining supplied.

Former Rain Insufficient

As important as the former rain is, it's not enough. We need the latter rain. Both are needed for Christian growth:

> "At no point in our experience can we dispense with the assistance of that which enables us to make the first start. The blessings received under the former rain are needful to us to the end. Yet these alone will not suffice. While we cherish the blessing of the early rain, we must not, on the other hand, lose sight of the fact that without the latter rain, *to fill out the ears and ripen the grain*, the harvest will not be ready for the sickle, and the labor of the sower will have been in vain." *Testimonies to Ministers,* 507, 508. Emphasis supplied.

The Other Extreme

Satan first tries to get some Christians to be lazy and unconcerned and thereby cause them to ignore the work of the former rain, the Holy Spirit's work upon the soul. He tries to get them to wait for the latter rain to cleanse them from known sins that should have been dealt with under the former rain.

On the other hand, many conservative Seventh-day Adventists have taught that which in effect conceals from our eyes the blessing God is waiting to bestow on us today, that is, the "perfecting latter rain."[2]

Many times Mrs. White has been quoted to say that absolutely every and all sins must be revealed, dealt with an overcome before the Holy Spirit in the latter rain can be bestowed upon the awaiting sinner.

With the quotations from *Testimonies to Ministers* cited above, it should be easy to see that this is not the case. Ellen White tells us we need to be ever "*daily advancing in the exemplification of the active Christian virtues;*" we must be "*living up to the light" that we have.*" We are to be clean from every known sin in our lives before we receive the refreshing of the latter rain, then the power of the Holy Spirit will be given to bring the seed to perfection, to bring His people to "*. . . The completion of the work of God's grace in the soul?*" At the time of the latter rain "*. . . The moral image of God is to be perfected in the character.*" *Testimonies to Ministers,* 506.

Tidings Out of the East

The position to which sinners must reach at the time of the outpouring of the Holy Spirit in the latter rain, is the point to where they have been forgiven every sin they're aware of (every known sin). At this point, they will have received the Holy Spirit into their lives under the power of the former rain. They're then prepared for the latter rain, if they're "living up to the light they have" and have no known sins to be forgiven and are neither cherishing nor participating in any known sins. They're holding nothing back from God. They're totally dedicated Christians, but still on the road to perfection, not actually having received it. They're truly converted, yet still not perfect, not yet totally sanctified.

Ellen White Dream

"In my dream a sentinel stood at the door of an important building, and asked everyone who came for entrance, "Have ye received the Holy Ghost?" A measuring-line was in his hand, and only very, very few were admitted into the building. "Your size as a human being is nothing," he said. "But if you have reached the full stature of a man in Christ Jesus, *according to the knowledge you have had*, you will receive an appointment to sit with Christ at the marriage supper of the Lamb; and through the eternal ages, you will never cease to learn of the blessings granted in the banquet prepared for you." "Review and Herald", April 11, 1899. Emphasis supplied.

The building portrayed here is the wedding hall of the marriage. Those that entered in entered into the judgment itself, the marriage supper. They must have on the wedding garment, provided them by the king. This is the righteousness of Christ. Only those who have been living up to the light, "according to the knowledge" they have had can enter in. Not all of their sins will have been revealed to them before their entrance into the judgment. They need only to have reached "the full stature of the man IN CHRIST, according to the knowledge [they] you have had." (Capitalization supplied.) They must be experiencing the former rain, trusting in the imputed righteousness of Christ. They will have the sanctifying power of God working in their lives. They aren't making excuses for sin, nor putting off the work of the Spirit in their lives. Nevertheless, they won't be perfect, although they will be seeking perfection, desiring it with all their hearts. They won't be neglecting to participate in daily sanctification. They are converted souls, desiring perfection to the glory of God.

We Must Understand This

When we understand what the latter rain does and that we must be on the road to the kingdom, living up to the light that we have, then God will judge us in the judgment according to His justifying grace, according to his own righteousness. We will not be judged according to our works, not by the work of our own effort nor even according to what the Holy Spirit has done in our lives.

We are totally judged and found righteous by the JUSTIFYING grace of God. This is why the 1888 message is justification by faith. This is why the third angel's message is justification by faith. This is why the third angel's message of the seal of God or the mark of the beast is justification by faith.

Knowing this, we can enter the most holy place with Jesus by faith. We can receive the unmerited cleansing of all our sins, the final atonement. Moses wrote concerning the Day of Atonement,

> "For on that day shall [the priest] make an atonement for you, to cleanse you, [that] ye may be clean from all your sins before the LORD. . .And he shall make an atonement for the holy sanctuary, and he shall make an atonement for the tabernacle of the congregation, and for the altar, and he shall make an atonement for the priests, and for all the people of the congregation. And this shall be an everlasting statute unto you, to make an atonement for the children of Israel for all their sins once a year. And he did as the LORD commanded Moses. " Leviticus 16:30, 33-34.

We need to come boldly before the throne today. We can have this boldness only by knowing that we are acceptable through the grace of God alone, justified by faith alone. Let us go forward *boldly*.

> "For we have not an high priest which cannot be touched with the feeling of our infirmities; but was in all points tempted like as [we are, yet] without sin. Let us therefore come boldly unto the throne of grace, that we may obtain mercy, and find grace to help in time of need." Hebrews 4:15, 16.

----

[1] Revelation 7:2

[2] "As we seek God for the Holy Spirit, it will work in us meekness, humbleness of mind, a conscious dependence upon God for the PERFECTING LATTER RAIN." "Review and Herald", March 2, 1897. Emphasis supplied.

Chapter 15
Eleventh Hour Christians

Do we have a dilemma here? What will happen to those who become Christians just before the close of probation? Will they be ready for heaven? The answer that's usually given is a valid one: "They will receive in a very short time the power to change their ways." That's exactly what's presented in the previous chapter. When the day-old Christian receives Christ, he's justified, and his Christian experience begins. God accepts him in Christ, and the gift of the Holy Spirit is given to him. This is the former or early rain.

It's a gift; we can't earn it today, tomorrow or at any time in the future. If we're living up to all the light that we have and if we're "in Christ," and if we're truly converted, we're as much deserving of the latter rain as anyone else. After all, those who are advanced in their Christian experience also received all that they have as a gift made possible by Christ's death. They too, have nothing to boast of except the cross. Their justification is a gift; their sanctification is also a gift. They have nothing of which to boast. The day-old Christian therefore, will also receive the latter rain, it's a gift.

The Work of a Lifetime

How long does it take to develop the Christian character to its fullest potential? Ellen White is often quoted where she says it's the work of a lifetime.[1] However, what if we had only ten years to develop Christian character before going to sleep in Jesus? Would that be enough time? Yes, we are accepted, justified in Christ, even though we haven't had the extended life to develop as some others who have been living the Christian life longer, forty or fifty years perhaps.

The thief on the cross will be in heaven even though he had only half a day under the former rain. He was a converted man, exercising faith in Jesus and was living up to all the light he had. The time for sanctification is our lifetimes, from the time we first believe to whenever we are placed in the ground, or when the latter rain comes to finish the work, "making man complete in Jesus Christ."[2]

Eleventh Hour Christians

In a parable, Jesus told of those who worked all day and received no more wages than those who started work near the end of the day. Was it fair? Does this parable apply to God's people at the end of time? What about the last minute Christian who joins the Lord's work just prior to the closing of probation? Will there be such people? Ellen White comments,

> "...when the crisis comes, many will be prepared to make right decisions even in the face of the formidable difficulties that will be brought about through the deceptive miracles of Satan. Although these will confess the truth and become workers with Christ at the eleventh hour, they will receive equal wages with those who have wrought through the whole day. There will be an army of steadfast believers who will stand as firm as a rock through the last test." "Review and Herald", Dec. 24, 1899. Underlining supplied.

Perfection before the Latter Rain

We have already dealt above with statements of Ellen White in *Testimonies to Ministers* concerning the latter rain and its effect on those who receive it. We read that the latter rain will perfect the character completely by restoring the image of God in His people. We learned that the latter rain is the "completion of the work of God's grace in the soul." The latter rain is called the "perfecting latter rain," and "The latter rain, falls near the close of the season, ripens the grain and prepares it for the sickle." Under the latter rain, we will be "transformed into likeness of Christ... The moral image is to be perfected in the character." This perfecting of the image of God in man will be by the power of the Holy Spirit. It's illustrated as the ripening of the harvest. At that time, the temple of man will be restored to the image of God, completely cleansed of all sin and sinfulness.

The statements in *Testimonies to Ministers* are clear. Who could read them and still believe that the saints of God will and must be absolutely, morally perfect before the latter rain falls? That being the case, how can the following statements which appear to say the opposite be harmonized? After reading the quotation below, please give some thought about how to make these apparently conflicting statements agree with what we read above.

> "Not one of us will ever receive the seal of God while our characters have one spot or stain upon them. It is left with us to remedy the defects in our characters, to

cleanse the soul temple of every defilement. Then the latter rain will fall upon us as the early rain fell upon the disciples on the Day of Pentecost." *Testimonies*, Vol. 5, 214.

The only way to bring such statements into one accord is by understanding the above statement is referring to known sins, and Ellen White is concerned about people who are lax about character development, waiting for the latter rain to do what the former rain should do. This is certainly true of the next quotation:

"The third angel's message is swelling into a loud cry, and you must not feel at liberty to neglect the present duty, and still entertain the idea that at some future time you will be the recipients of great blessing, when without any effort on your part a wonderful revival will take place. Today you are to give yourselves to God, that He may make of you vessels unto honor, and meet for His service. Today you are to give yourself to God, that you may be emptied of self, emptied of envy, jealousy, evil surmising, strife, everything that shall be dishonoring to God. Today you are to have your vessel purified that it may be ready for the heavenly dew, ready for the showers of the latter rain; for the latter rain will come, and the blessing of God will fill every soul that is purified from every defilement. It is our work today to yield our souls to Christ, that we may be fitted for the time of refreshing from the presence of the Lord-- fitted for the baptism of the Holy Spirit." "Review and Herald", March 22, 1892. *Selected Messages*, Book 1, 190, 191.

Why would anyone be waiting idly for the latter rain to do a great work in him or her? Simply because that's indeed the Holy Spirit's work, to do a completing work in us. However, we aren't to wait for the latter rain to do the work of the former rain. We must be at work even now to have our souls cleansed of every defilement, and then the latter rain can fall and finish the work of grace in the soul. Many are neglecting this work:

"I saw that many were neglecting the preparation so needful and were looking to the time of "refreshing" and the "latter rain" to fit them to stand in the day of the Lord and to live in His sight." *Early Writings*, 71.

Here again these people are looking for the latter rain to do a work they need to do under the former rain. Next, Ellen White speaks of the time of trouble, after the "refreshing" had prepared God's people for the time when there will be no mediator. She tells us it's important they not neglect the former rain, expecting the latter rain to do what they have neglected.

"Oh, how many I saw in the time of trouble without a shelter! They had neglected the needful preparation; therefore they could not receive the refreshing that all must have to fit them to live in the sight of a holy God. Those who refuse to be

Tidings Out of the East

hewed by the prophets and fail to purify their souls in obeying the whole truth, and who are willing to believe that their condition is far better than it really is, will come up to the time of the falling of the plagues, and then see that they needed to be hewed and squared for the building. But there will be no time then to do it and no Mediator to plead their cause before the Father. Before this time the awfully solemn declaration has gone forth, "He that is unjust, let him be unjust still: and he which is filthy, let him be filthy still: and he that is righteous, let him be righteous still: and he that is holy, let him be holy still." *Early Writings*, 71.

The continuation of this statement in *Early Writings* gives us the idea that the saints will be sinless before the latter rain will fall. It indeed appears that way, but taking other quotations in mind, we should conclude that here again she's talking about known sins, besetting sins. She's not referring to yet unrevealed sins, and her emphasis in this statement is to get God's people off their couches of apathy and onto the road of reform and character development. The danger here addressed is laxness in character reform and the waiting for the latter rain to do the former rain's work.

Please take note that at the end of the quotation below, Ellen White talks about "that preparation necessary to enable us to stand in the battle in the day of the Lord." This is the latter rain and is clearly character development, the "perfecting latter rain," that ". . . ripens the grain and prepares it for the sickle." *Testimonies to Ministers*, 506-509.

"I saw that none could share the 'refreshing' unless they obtain the victory over every besetment, over pride, selfishness, love of the world, and over every wrong word and action. We should, therefore, be drawing nearer and nearer to the Lord and be earnestly seeking that preparation necessary to enable us to stand in the battle in the day of the Lord. Let all remember that God is holy and that none but holy beings can ever dwell in His presence." *Early Writings*, 71.

He's Patiently Waiting

God is waiting to give us a special blessing in the gift of his Holy Spirit at the time of the latter rain. It's the blessing of the judgment. We pass the judgment as we look to Christ in the most holy place of the sanctuary; He is presenting his blood for our sins. This is the third angel's message. This is justification by faith. To date, we have not realized the blessing God has for us. We need to exercise the faith necessary; then we can receive the latter rain. At the same time, we shouldn't be idly waiting by for the latter rain to do what was neglected under the former rain. Nevertheless, there's a great blessing of "spiritual grace" in the latter rain. The pen of inspiration tells us,

"But near the close of earth's harvest, a special bestowal of spiritual grace is promised to prepare the church for the coming of the Son of man. This outpouring of the Spirit is likened to the falling of the latter rain . . ." *Acts of the Apostles*, p. 54, 55. Emphasis supplied.

---

[1] *Selected Messages*, Book 1, 318
[2] *Testimonies to Ministers*, 507.

Chapter 16
The Missing Link

The Lord should have come shortly after 1844, and then shortly after 1888, yet both times we missed the chance. We Seventh-day Adventists rejected a "most precious message." Forty years later in 1928 there was another emphasis on justification by faith and then again 40 more years after that in about 1968 with Wieland and Short and their book, *1888 Re-examined*. Others at that same time were presenting light on the sanctuary truth. Today, more than forty years later, 2008 plus, surely, there must be another emphasis on justification by faith and the third angel's message.

I attended the 1888 Conference Seminar in June of 2012 in Gentry, Arkansas. I was hoping to find out what we are missing in our understanding. I thought that if the message of 1888 was being discussed at this Arkansas 1888 Conference, they must have the answer to why we have missed so many opportunities over the past 160 years.

At one meeting, during a question and answer sessions, I explained this long period of 160 years and then asked the presenter if he knew what was missing. I asked him if was aware of any "missing link." He was very brief in his answer. He said, "No." Then he looked into the audience where most of the other presenters were. He asked them my question. Not a soul said a thing. There was no further discussion on it, and we went on to the next question. After that, I concluded that I wouldn't find the answer at that seminar. I wondered why they seemed so uninterested in finding the answer. No one said a thing to me about it later. Apparently, I had failed to raise any interest.

Personally, I believe that question to be of the utmost importance. We should all be searching for the answer. For us, the members of the Seventh-day Adventist Church, we who were put here to bring about the final generation, this should be our constant study. We need to know that missing link.

The Final Generation, When?

What makes the final generation the final generation? I asked that question to a conference president back in 1977. Our discussion went something like this:

> Q: How will the final generation be different from any other?
> A: They will be without sin in their lives.
> Q: Why will the final generation have no sin in their lives?
> A: They will have put away all their sins.
> Q: Why will the final generation have put away all their sins and not so any generation before them?
> A: They work harder at it by submitting their lives more completely to God.
> Q: Why does the final generation submit itself more completely to God?
> A: They pray more, study more and worship more.
> Q: Why do they pray more, study more and worship more?
> A: They try harder.
> Q: Why does the final generation try harder?
> A. . . .

By this time, the pastor was either beginning to see he didn't really have the answer, or possibly, he was just tired of my questions. He had a puzzled look on his face; he likely realized he really didn't know. He didn't answer me to my satisfaction, nor did I think I had the correct answer either. I asked these questions because I needed to know. I wasn't trying to put him in a corner.

I believed the answer to why the final generation becomes the final generation is tantamount to entering the final stages of God's plan for that generation. I thought something was missing. I was searching for the missing link.

Does the final generation just try harder? Do they know more? What's the ingredient the makes them the final generation and hasn't made the final generation out of any previous generation?

What We Need is Present Truth

"There are many precious truths contained in the Word of God, but it is present truth that the flock needs now. I have seen the danger of the messengers running off from the important points of present truth, to dwell upon subjects that are not calculated to unite the flock and sanctify the soul. Satan will here take every possible advantage to injure the cause.

"But such subjects as the sanctuary, in connection with the 2300 days, the commandments of God and the faith of Jesus, are perfectly calculated to explain the past Advent movement and show what our present position is, establish the faith of the doubting, and give certainty to the glorious future. These, I have frequently seen, were the principal subjects on which the messengers should dwell." *Early Writings*, 63.

The missing link is clearly explained in the above quotations on present truth. However, what is the sanctuary truth? Is it so clear? Possibly, it has been misrepresented or misunderstood. Do we really know what present truth is?

Something Missing in Daniel and Revelation?

"When the books of Daniel and Revelation are better understood, believers will have an entirely different religious experience. They will be given such glimpses of the open gates of heaven that heart and mind will be impressed with the character that all must develop in order to realize the blessedness which is to be the reward of the pure in heart. The Lord will bless all who will seek humbly and meekly to understand that which is revealed in the Revelation. This book contains so much that is large with immortality and full of glory that all who read and search it earnestly receive the blessing to those 'that hear the words of this prophecy, and keep those things which are written therein.' One thing will certainly be understood from the study of Revelation--that the connection between God and His people is close and decided." *The Faith I Live By*, 345.

Has Daniel been understood completely? How many of us can explain Revelation from beginning to end?[1] In order to understand what might be missing, we might have to give up some of our most cherished ideas, some that we have studied extensively to where we are sure we will never change our minds on these issues.

Two Choices

When I was a colporteur years ago, I learned to give the customers two choices when I made my final appeal. Both choices were in my favor, that is, no matter which of the two choices the customer made, I still had a sale. I never gave the choice of buying the books or not buying them. Instead, I asked which set or combination of books the customer would like to purchase.

Satan is no less than a super salesman, who, when possible, gives us two or more wrong choices. Ellen White mentions this technique in *Great Controversy*. Concerning the papacy and its methods and speaking of salvation, she says:

> "The papacy is well adapted to meet the wants of all these. It is prepared for two classes of mankind, embracing nearly the whole world--those who would be saved by their merits, and those who would be saved in their sins. Here is the secret of its power." *Great Controversy*, 572.

Satan through the Papacy offers us two choices. One is a way to *earn* our way to heaven with works, if we desire that method. I wonder; do we practice this when we say we have to be perfect before we can receive the benefits of the final atonement, that is, when we say we have to be perfect before the latter rain can fall? This leads us to a hard, legalistic style of life, never knowing if we have done enough and ever hoping the judgment will not come in our lifetime. This was my story, until I understood justification by faith as it really is. Recently, many simple try to flee from the thought of a judgment or the latter rain or even last day events.

On the other hand, if we wish to avoid obedience, or to avoid what we might think is legalism, we might wish to feel completely free of any obligation to the law of God. This is known as "cheap grace." Satan offers two wrong choices, while the truth is left along the side of the road with most people choosing one of Satan's two choices, both wrong.

If You Love Me, Keep My Commandments

The truth is that we should obey, not because we're hoping to be saved, or justified by obedience. Instead, we should obey because we love God and love obedience. Because we love Him, should be our reason to keep His commandments. Since our day of conversion, we have become more like Christ, and our obedience is more out of love and more out of a desire to bring Him glory. We are justified by Christ's life and His death, never by the works done in our own power or even the works of God in us. This is the third angel's message, the message of 1888, justification by faith.

Before we can receive the final atonement and reach the position God intends for us to attain, we must understand and take hold of some essential teachings concerning the final generation and the complete restoration of the moral image of God in us. This final work is the complete fulfillment of the new covenant promise. Jeremiah and Isaiah have revealed the promise to us:

> "In those days, and in that time, saith the Lord, the iniquity of Israel shall be sought for, and there shall be none; and the sins of Judah, and they shall not be found." Jeremiah 31:34; 50:20.

"In that day shall the branch of the Lord be beautiful and glorious, and the fruit of the earth shall be excellent and comely for them that are escaped of Israel. And it shall come to pass, that he that is left in Zion, and he that remaineth in Jerusalem, shall be called holy, even every one that is written among the living in Jerusalem." Isaiah 4:2, 3.

Sister White tells us we must enter into the final atonement that's symbolized by the work of Jesus in the most holy of the heavenly sanctuary. Entering in isn't done in actuality, but by faith. We don't actually go there.

"Now Christ is in the heavenly sanctuary. And what is He doing? Making atonement for us, cleansing the sanctuary from the sins of the people. Then we must enter by faith into the sanctuary with Him, we must commence the work in the sanctuary of our souls. We are to cleanse ourselves from all defilement." *1888*, 127.

"Let us enter by faith the holy of holies, and hold communion with our heavenly Father and with our Redeemer, the Saviour of sinners, who will wash us and make us white in His blood." 20 Manuscript Release, 153.

How Do We Enter By Faith?

Do we simply acknowledge we believe that the sanctuary is there and that in 1844 Jesus entered the most holy place, leaving the holy place? Is that entering by faith? No, it's much more. Entering by faith means understanding what Jesus is doing there and co-operating with Him in His work. This is what it means to enter by faith. This is the missing link. It's found in Daniel and Revelation, in the sanctuary, in the new covenant promise.

How does justification by faith apply to our entering into the most holy place? It's simply this. When we enter, knowing that we are acceptable to God and justified by Him only on the merits of Jesus justifying act of living and dying for us, we can stand before God without fear, knowing that in Him we are accepted, justified.

Many in our past history, and some historic Adventists today still believe we have to be perfect before we can enter and receive the blessings of the final atonement, the most holy place experience. However, not so. Trying to get God to accept us in the final work of salvation, the Day of Atonement, by looking at what we have done in the flesh, either with or without the work of the Holy Spirit, is a subtle form of justification by works. [2]

How do we enter by faith? First, by understanding what Jesus is waiting to do for His people. Then, we ask Him for forgiveness and to accept us in the name of Jesus, justified by His life and His death alone. When enough of His followers do so, then He will pour out the latter rain, first to the 144,000 and later to the great multitude. This will be the perfecting, sealing later rain. This will be the fulfillment of the new covenant promise, the "completion of the work of God's grace in the soul." It will prepare a people to stand before God without a mediator [3] through the time of trouble. Then, Jesus will come. This is the good news of the gospel. God is Love. He is waiting eagerly to bless us. Today let's look to Jesus in the most holy.

This Is the Gospel, Good News

This is good news. We can come boldly into the judgment today, if we have confessed our sins as they have been made known to us and we are in this saving relationship with Jesus Christ. This can't be emphasized too much. We must be in a daily walk with Jesus, not refusing the pleading of the Holy Spirit nor purposefully carrying on with any known sin. We must be born again.

When we understand what Jesus is waiting to do for us in the most holy of the heavenly sanctuary, we can receive great blessings in the judgment. To believe that we must totally overcome all sins, known and unknown, before the latter rain can fall, only delays the judgment even farther into the future. This has been our problem before and since 1888. The message of 1888 was justification by faith. We must understand how the third angel's message is justification by faith and that we can enter the final judgment and receive the latter rain, being justified by faith alone. God says, "all things are ready, come to the marriage."[4] We must believe this and enter by faith.

Tidings Out of the East

The sealing of the 144,000, brought about by the acceptance of the third angel's message, justification by faith alone, is the *tidings out of the east*. The latter rain perfects and seals us; God's promise to give us the latter rain is the *tidings out of the east*. The new covenant promise, which takes away all our sins, is the *tidings out of the east*. The *tidings out of the east* is God's fulfillment of the plan He put in place many years ago to completely redeem us from the effects of Adam's sin. It restores the people, the sanctuary, the kingdom and the king.

Praise be to God, for God is Love. All things are ready, come to the marriage.

---

[1] For a comprehensive, yet simple way to understand the Book of Revelation, please read another book by this same author, *Restoring the Holy of Holies* –

Revelation – A Seven Act Play, available at all books store chains and Internet book sellers.

² For a more comprehensive look at justification by faith and the sanctuary message, in conjunction with the 1888 message, please read *Restoring Ta Hagia Restoring the Image of God in His People,* by this same author.

³ Without a mediator does not mean Jesus or the Father has left us, only that we no longer need a mediator to deal with our sins in the sanctuary. God walked with Adam and Even before sin, yet they didn't have a mediator, because they were without sin. What was lost in Eden will eventually be restored in God's people in the end of time.

⁴ Matthew 22:4

Other Books by This Author

Restoring the Holy of Holies - Revelation - A Seven-act Play

This book is for every Christian. A fair amount of Bible knowledge is required. It contains the same message of the final generation, 144,000 and great multitude, but without quotations from Ellen White.

Omega Now - A Most Startling Heresy
The Omega of apostasy is here. We are at the end of time. Many will be deceived who are only surface readers, allowing others to tell them what truth is. W must know for ourselves.

Restoring Ta Hagia - Recreating the Image of God in His People

The word *Ta Hagia* is found two places in the New Testament, one place it is translated, *saints*. The other is the *sanctuary*. The saints are living sanctuaries, awaiting the final atonement, but how will it be realized? We have been waiting more than 160 years.

www.ingramcontent.com/pod-product-compliance
Lightning Source LLC
Chambersburg PA
CBHW071300040426
42444CB00009B/1809